The
New
Teacher's
Survival
Guide

The
New
Teacher's
Survival
Guide

MARILYN NATHAN

**KOGAN
PAGE**

London • Philadelphia

First published in 1995

Kogan Page Limited
120 Pentonville Road
London N1 9JN

British Library Cataloguing in Publication Data

A CIP record for this book is available from the British Library.

ISBN 0 7494 1676 9

Typeset by BookEns Ltd, Royston, Herts.
Printed and bound in Great Britain by Biddles Ltd,
Guildford and King's Lynn

Contents

Acknowledgements

I should like to thank two members of the staff of Doctor Challoner's High School, Ann Flaherty and Sue Oldfield, who have been working with me to develop mentoring in school, and who both contributed to this book, particularly to Chapter 3, 'The Logistics of Classroom Life'. When 'we' is used in the text, it is not royal, but means that I have discussed the matter with my colleagues and that this is our concerted opinion. I should also like to thank Leigh Lewis for all the help he gave me in preparing this book for publication, particularly for his help with the diagrams printing and graphics.

Introduction

What Is This Book About?

This book is intended as an introduction to teaching for new entrants to the profession. In it we try to provide the kind of information, advice and ideas you could find useful if you are taking up a teaching post for the first time. In the past teachers were simply expected to manage, to muddle through, to find their feet in their own way – or not, as the case may be. Teaching was always a hard profession to enter; now it has become an even harder one, because the demands on teachers in recent years have escalated with the vast number of new initiatives schools have had to undertake, along with an increased emphasis on quality teaching and accountability. Your new school should have a member of staff who is responsible for the induction of all new members of staff, but the quality, let alone the availability of his/her advice and support, will vary according to the ability and interest of the individual concerned, and to a large extent you will find yourself on your own to sink or swim. A survival guide for new teachers could therefore provide you with some of the support and guidance you need in the first few terms on the job.

The question this book attempts to answer is: *'How do I become an effective teacher?'*

- It analyses the teaching skills you need.
- It explores possible methods of handling situations you may have to face.
- It provides suggestions about how to manage the various relationships with pupils, parents, colleagues etc. which teaching entails.
- It analyses and discusses the duties and responsibilities you have as a teacher and provides advice about how to manage them.

The aim is to provide you with a compendium of information and advice. This book does not seek to be original, but to gather together in a convenient and user-friendly format ideas and suggestions that you can apply in the classroom. This means that this is essentially a book about good practice. This does not mean that there is no theory included, rather that it is integrated into the discussion of the particular issue and that the ideas are introduced or illustrated by specific examples or case studies. Where we are indebted to a particular work or project for focusing our thoughts on an issue, we have highlighted this in the chapter concerned so that you know where to go for further reading.

What makes a good teacher is a question that any new entrant to the profession will think about a lot and we discuss it fully in the last chapter. Most of us start by thinking of teachers we have known who are good or bad. This book accepts that some good teachers are born and not made, but we profoundly believe that most of us are capable of improving our teaching and that a compendium which helps us reflect on our practice by describing and analysing situations with which we can identify could help us pre-empt some problems and deal with others as they arise. Some of the advice may seem self-evident. This is intentional – we should never overlook the obvious, especially as under the pressure of managing a whole range of different things at the same time, one crucial element may be forgotten. For this reason a number of checklists or hints for managing different activities have been included – we have used 'the useful tips for teaching' approach. This kind of checklist is intended as a starting point for you: some general advice which could help you to get things right, but it is not a blueprint for success. Your actions must be determined by the particular circumstances with which you will have to deal. Fail-safe prescriptions are difficult because of the varied and disparate nature of any group of learners and the individuality of the teacher, but what we can do is to provide you with examples of strategies which you can apply – how you interpret or use them is up to you.

Who Is It For?

We hope that four broad groups of teachers will find this book useful:

New Entrants to the Profession

This book aims to provide advice and guidance for new teachers in their first year of teaching. Most of these new teachers will be fresh from college and about to start their first job. Some chapters, such as *'Before you start'*, are specifically geared to helping you make a good start. Some new teachers will be late entrants to the profession, making the difficult transfer to a completely different career, and others will be returning to the profession after a gap. For all these 'new' teachers, this book will try to provide the practical guidance you will need in the difficult period when you first take up the post.

Teachers who Want to Reflect on their Practice

A lot of this book is about good practice in teaching and one of the characteristics of an effective teacher is that s/he never stops learning about how to do it better. We shall pose some key questions and outline some approaches and strategies you can consider and possibly adapt to your own needs. In this way we hope to help colleagues reflect on their own practice and evaluate the ideas and methods that they are using.

Student Teachers

Students are now expected to spend about 70 per cent of their time training on the job in schools, so right from the start of this training they need to know how schools operate. We hope to make this book coincide with the type of course student teachers are now following and provide the kind of advice and suggestions which will help them survive their lengthy teaching practices and become effective teachers.

Teacher Tutors, Mentors, Professional Tutors, College Tutors

This book could also operate as a course or reference book for teacher tutors or mentors trying to support newly qualified teachers or students. The case studies and situations we discuss and analyse and the strategies and approaches we suggest could form the basis of a series of tutorial sessions.

How To Use It

In this book you will find practical advice about how to go about most of the duties you will have to undertake as a new teacher. The list below indicates some of the areas which are likely to be priorities for you and there are chapters or sections on each of them:

- managing the transition from student to teacher
- understanding how the school operates
- what it means to be a tutor
- class control and discipline
- classroom management
- how to improve techniques
- marking and recording performance.

Integrated through the book are case studies which will give you the chance to consider and work on typical teaching situations or reflect on issues. We shall pose and discuss a lot of the problems that are likely to arise and suggest some approaches and strategies you could adopt or adapt. What we cannot give you is an absolute blueprint for successful teaching, as no such thing exists. There is no absolutely right way to teach and a great deal depends on how the individual teacher interprets and applies the techniques and ideas suggested here.

One approach to this book is to read it through from beginning to end. Alternatively, and perhaps more usefully, you can dip into it for specific advice on an aspect of your role in which you feel you need information or support. If you are going to dip into particular sections, you will find it useful to know how we use the case study material. In this volume we shall continue to use the same approach as we have used in the other Survival Guides.

Case Studies

All the chapters include some case studies. They are numbered within each chapter. Many of the case studies, though not all, focus on an imaginary school called Bestwick Park High School, an urban, multicultural, mixed comprehensive school. Even if your school is not urban, or multicultural or even comprehensive, you are still likely to find more than an echo of your own situation in the Bestwick Park case studies, and that the issues outlined will generally have a relevance to all school situations.

Occasionally – as for example in Chapter 10 – the case studies will run in sequence, but usually each is complete on its own.

The case studies can be used both for group discussion and for individual reflection. Some case studies will be analysed for you so that you can see possible solutions, which themselves can serve to focus discussion; others are posed as problems for you to solve.

There are three categories of case study:

1. *Exemplars.* These are examples of how things are done, such as a sample instruction sheet on how to complete your register. They are included to help you interpret the kind of information that you may be given.
2. *For reflection.* These case studies, which either describe a situation or make some points about an issue, invite you to think about the issue raised, possibly linked to some discussion points.
3. *For action.* These case studies set out a situation, provide you with some information and invite you to consider what action you would take, eg, by putting you in the place of a Newly Qualified Teacher dealing with a difficult pastoral problem and asking you what issues are involved and what steps you would take to deal with the problem.

CHAPTER 1

Before you start

You have been appointed to your first teaching post. Starting out in a new school is a daunting experience for any teacher and especially hard if this is your first teaching post. Naturally you want to make a good start. First impressions count for a lot. If you want to establish yourself as an effective and capable teacher from the word 'go', you will have to look and sound as if you know what you are doing. Making a good initial impression will also help you build up your own confidence at a time when this will matter, so what do you do?

Make Arrangements to Visit the School

You will want to visit the school at least once before you take up the post. It will help you to become familiar with a strange building and provide an opportunity for you to gather some of the information you will need. How many visits will you need to make? Two visits would be ideal, one shortly after the successful interview, to get to know the department, and the second towards the end of the term before you take up the post, in order to firm up on what you have to do to prepare for the new job and to collect textbooks and other things that you might need. But don't worry if this proves impossible; it is often the case that people are simply located too far away to visit more than once. The important thing is that you get the most you can out of your visit.

What Kind of Questions Will you Need to Ask?

- Will the school be open in the holidays if I want to come in?

- Do I have to come into school on the day before the beginning of term?
- Where is the staff cloakroom?
- What are the arrangements for tea and coffee?
- What are the conventions about dress — do I have to look smart?
- What happens on the first day — will I have to teach some lessons?
- Where will I find communications or messages — is there a staff notice board?
- Will I have to be a form tutor?
- Will there be a lot of meetings after school?
  (From a new teacher's list of questions.)

These questions indicate some areas where one new teacher did not know what to expect and about which s/he felt apprehensive. A lot of the questions concerned very basic information, yet not knowing what is expected can make you feel extremely insecure. You will probably be able to think of other similar questions to which you need answers. Writing these down helped this Newly Qualified Teacher (NQT) to clarify the information she wanted and you may find it useful to adopt this strategy.

To make the best use of the visit, you need to be clear about what you want to know. You will want information about:

- how the school functions and its procedures
- any responsibilities and duties you may have
- what you are expected to teach.

Finding Out How the School Functions

A good school should send you a pack of information, but if it doesn't, you will have to take the initiative. To get information about the school, telephone or write to the school secretary and ask for such things as a list of the holiday dates, a chart of how the school day is organized, a room plan of the school, and a copy of the prospectus for the coming year. These things will give you some initial information about the school and help you find your way around.

The Staff Handbook

If there is a good staff handbook, it will become your most

valuable asset. Ignore all the jokes you may hear about it being fodder for the filing cabinet; read it carefully and refer to it frequently during your first term. It will provide you with a compendium of information about how the school operates. It will give you a good indication of how formal, bureaucratic or casual the ethos is; more importantly, it will spell out and give you detailed instructions as to how to go about a lot of the daily tasks, which may not be clear to you. It also saves someone the trouble of having to explain everything to you individually. Knowing what is in the handbook could save you from the weary, irritable, but totally predictable retort from whichever senior member of staff you accost with your urgent problem – 'It's in the staff handbook – haven't you read it?' It could even make it possible for you to reply, 'I have read the handbook, and it does not tell me how to do this. . .'

CASE STUDY 1.1. FOR REFLECTION

From the Staff Handbook

Perhaps we should start this case study with a warning. The language and style of the handbook is rarely user-friendly, and locating the relevant paragraph or section can itself present you with some problems as you cannot rely on it having an index, and the organization of the materials included can be idiosyncratic in the extreme. Persevere however, because a lot of the information you want will be in the handbook, if you can only manage to find it!

Several of the questions any new teacher will have will be about what will happen on the first day of term. The examples from the Bestwick Park staff handbook given below will provide answers to a lot of these questions.

Example 1: The First Day of Term

8.40	New pupils assemble in the hall except year 7, who go to the dining hall to be received by their year head and be put into forms.
8.40	All other pupils should go to their old form rooms to be received by last year's form tutor. Go to the hall for assembly when the bell rings.
8.55–9.05	Assembly in the hall

At the end of assembly, form lists will be read by the deputy head and forms should leave the hall with their new tutor and go to their new form room.

9.05–11.20 Form time

During form time:

1. Check names and dates of birth on the form list, correct addresses and telephone numbers, and send the amended list to the office immediately. Except in the case of Year 12, write up registers. Year 12 tutors should keep temporary registers for a few days until lists are confirmed.
2. Issue the form timetable. Each pupil should make him/herself a neat copy. There should also be a copy on the form notice board.
3. Collect school fund money and send it to the bursar's office in the bag provided before the end of form time.
4. Check lunch numbers and send the form captain to enter them in the lunch register in the dining room. Send a pupil to collect all the stationery your form requires, including rough books. It will be available from the stationery cupboard from 9.30. Collect any information which matron may have asked for. She will put a notice in your form register to say what she wants.
5. Elect form officials – form captain, games monitors, homework and subject monitors, charity, stationery and tidiness monitors and a school council representative. In Year 7 officials are elected after two weeks to give pupils time to get to know one another.
6. Go over the rules and remind pupils about the school Code of Conduct.
7. Go through the uniform list and carry out a uniform check.
8. Make sure that the pupils know the rotas for assembly and lunch and understand the fire and emergency regulations.
9. Give out bus passes, rough books and the homework timetable. Explain it clearly to the pupils. See that all the pupils have a notebook in which to record homework and that they have copied the homework timetable into the front of this notebook.
10. Forms will be sent for in turn so that they can be given their cloakroom places.

11.20 Normal timetable will commence, ie, period 4.

This set of instructions from the staff handbook is very precise. It tells you very clearly what the arrangements for the first day are, how you link up with your new tutor group and what you have to do with them during form time. It also clearly answers the question, 'Will I have to teach any lessons on the first day?' In this school the teaching timetable begins at period 4 after all the form business has been completed.

Example 2: Arriving and Leaving

Staff should arrive in school well in time for registration at 8.40 am unless they are on early morning duty, in which case they should arrive by 8.30 am.

If you intend to leave the building during a free period, please check that you are not required to cover a class for an absent teacher, and please sign the sheet in the staffroom (on the staff notice board) so that we know that you have gone off the premises.

If you are free last period in the afternoon (period 8) you may leave provided that you have checked with the deputy head that you are not needed for cover. Please sign out in the same way as you do when you go out during a free period.

This example indicates that you are expected to be in school before registration, but isn't prescriptive about how long before. It spells out, however, what time you have to be in your classroom in the morning. It also tells you that you can go out of school during the day if you are free and that it is acceptable to leave early if you are free for the last period in the afternoon. Schools do differ about how they treat the staff, so it is important to check what the acceptable practice is. Bestwick Park has clearly decided to offer staff the opportunity to go off site as long as they sign out; other schools may be less generous in this respect.

Example 3: Staff Meetings

Autumn term: in the afternoon of the day before term begins – starting time 1.30 pm.

Other terms: On the first Wednesday in each half term at 3.30 pm. Guillotine is at 5.00 pm.

Weekly staff meetings, which are mainly used for briefing and information exchange, are held on Wednesday mornings at 8.35 am. Other meetings – heads of department, department, heads of year, year meetings, etc. – are held at 3.30 pm on Wednesdays. A rota is drawn up and it can be found in the section of the calendar entitled 'Wednesday meeting list'. The calendar is circulated termly. These meetings take place in directed time. Guillotine is at 5.00 pm.

This example provides the answer to the question about how many after-school meetings you are likely to have to attend. As a new teacher you will be involved in staff meetings, departmental meetings and year or tutors' meetings. Your school may also have a faculty system. In Bestwick Park High School, a decision has been made to concentrate all meetings on the same day each week – Wednesday. This is the simplest system as it is the easiest to remember, but not all schools work to this plan. Some will have different types of meetings on different evenings, so check the handbook carefully so that you understand what system is being used. At Bestwick Park it is clearly stated that all the meetings are in directed time, ie that they are compulsory and all teachers have to attend. This is likely to be the case at any school, but at Bestwick Park there is a guillotine, ie it is made clear that meetings should not last beyond 5.00 pm. Check to see whether this procedure operates in your new school, because knowing the precise timespan of meetings will help you avoid making other commitments that could overlap.

Finding Out About Your Duties and Responsibilities

The best source of information about your duties and responsibilities will be your job description, so if you are not given one by your head of department (HOD) or by the headteacher, make sure you ask for one. It should spell out what is expected of you. An example of a main-grade teacher's job description is given below in Case study no. 1.2. Read it through carefully and see that you understand it. The job description in the case study has a long list of tasks because it goes step-by-step through the main aspects of your job as a classroom teacher. You will notice, however, that the lengthy list has been split into three sections:

■ *Principal responsibilities* – this section refers to your duties as a classroom teacher, particularly to your preparation of and teaching of lessons and the marking of work. Some job descriptions will include specific requirements about your subject at the end of this section.
■ *Additional responsibilities* – eg as a form tutor.
■ *General duties* – this section is about staff duties, ie times when you have to supervise pupils when not in the classroom, such as at break or lunchtime or when pupils are waiting for buses or coaches.

As you acquire additional responsibilities, they will be added to your generic job description or the list will be amended. The last paragraph in the section headed 'general duties' provides a mechanism for reviewing or modifying your duties. Your job description could also form the basis for any appraisal you may have in the future. It is an important document for you, so make sure that it is satisfactory. If there is anything in it which worries you or that you don't understand, raise the matter either with your HOD or with the member of staff, probably one of the deputy heads, who is in charge of the induction of new staff.

CASE STUDY 1.2. EXEMPLAR

Bestwick Park High School
Teacher of .... Main Grade

Principal responsibilities
Under the direction of the head of department
a)   To contribute to the teaching of ...
b)   To participate in the development of appropriate syllabuses, materials and schemes of work.

These responsibilities should be met by working to the guidelines set out:

■   To prepare and organize lessons in accordance with the National Curriculum or an agreed syllabus (as appropriate) and using teaching strategies and methods formulated in departmental meetings to an agreed schedule.
■   To arrive punctually at lessons and to expect and ensure well-disciplined lessons.
■   To end lessons punctually and to dismiss pupils, in an orderly way.
■   To set and mark homework regularly according to school policy and in a style agreed within the department.
■   To carry out class assessments of pupils' progress and complete records according to agreed departmental grading policy.
■   To collaborate in the setting and marking of examination papers requested by the head of department.
■   To complete reports or profiles on pupils' progress and achievements for the information of parents in accordance with school policy.
■   To attend parents' evenings as required.
■   To assist the progress of pupils by encouragement and praise

whenever possible and to be constructive in any comments and guidance.

■ To discuss with heads of department any pupil whose work is a cause for concern and to decide in consultation with him/her any further action.

■ To attend staff and departmental meetings as required.

■ To contribute to curriculum development and to maintain specialist expertise by being aware of recent developments in the subject.

Additional responsibilities

■ To be a form tutor of an assigned form and to carry out related duties in accordance with the general job description of a form tutor.

General duties

■ To carry out a share of supervisory duties in accordance with the published rota.

■ To participate in appropriate meetings with colleagues and parents relative to the above duties.

Note

1. The above responsibilities are subject to the general duties and responsibilities contained in the statement of Conditions of Employment.

2. This job description allocates duties and responsibilities but does not direct the particular amount of time to be spent on carrying them out and no part of it may be so construed. In allocating time to the performance of duties and responsibilities, the postholder must use directed time in accordance with the school's published Time Budget Policy and have regard to clause 4(I) (f) of a Teacher's Conditions of Employment.

3. This job description is not necessarily a comprehensive definition of the post. It will be reviewed regularly, if possible, not less than once a year, and it may be subject to modification or amendment at any time after consultation with the holder of the post.

Finding Out What you are Expected to Teach

You will want to know two main things:

■ What the content of the courses is that you will have to teach.

■ For which groups of pupils you will be responsible.

To learn about the content of the courses you will have to teach, you should start by reading the syllabuses. As well as the external examination board syllabuses, such as the GCSE, A Level or GNVQ, your department should have a departmental syllabus and schemes of work for each year group. Your HOD should provide you with copies of each of these when you visit the school and s/he should spend some time going through them with you to see that you understand what is required. Keep asking if you are not given this information, as it is essential that you have it.

Collect a copy of each of the main textbooks or worksheets that you will be using in the first term, so that you can become familiar with them and work out where and how you will use them. This will help you to know where they do not meet your needs and where you will have to supplement them with other materials. Spend some time learning where things are in the textbook so that you are visibly familiar with it when you have to use it with the pupils. This strategy will make it easier for you to use the books with confidence in the first few days and will help you make a favourable impression, as the pupils will believe that you know what you are about.

Your personal timetable will be given to you either directly by the deputy head or more likely by your HOD, who will have been given all the timetables for the department. How soon before the end of the summer term you receive it will depend on the complexities of the school's timetable and the skill of the timetabler. There could be alterations at a late date, so don't expect everything to be cut and dried on your first visit. Just make sure that you arrange a mechanism for receiving the information you need as soon as it is available.

Some of the information, particularly the timetable, may seem like it's written in a foreign language because of the abbreviations, initials and codes used. Your HOD should explain to you what it all means, so that you understand which groups you have been given, what the signs are for a teaching group, which number or letter is the room and whether it is a mixed ability, streamed or setted group and whether you have a reasonable range of classes. The time should be gone when the newest teacher got all the worst classes, but do look at class size because it will indicate how heavy your marking load will be, and the number of different classes or year groups will be an indication of the volume of preparation you will have to undertake.

If set lists have been printed and are available for the coming year, it is a sensible idea to enter the names of your teaching group in your mark book before the start of term, as this will save you an onerous task in the first few days when you are likely to have a lot of other jobs to do. You will find the first few days in a new job stressful and it makes a lot of sense to look for ways to lessen the pressures by doing some of the jobs in advance and before term starts.

Some Thoughts for the First Few Days

- Everyone is entitled to some mistakes – even a new teacher!
- It took God a week to make the world ....
- If you don't take your own mistakes too seriously, others will laugh with you and not at you.
- You are not on your own – if in doubt, ask advice!

Your First Lesson with a Class – Some Points to Think About

- What would you like to know about the class in advance – why?
- What sort of topic or theme will you choose for the first lesson – why?
- What teaching strategies/method of delivery (eg, chalk and talk, group work, etc.) will you employ – why?
- When should you plan and prepare the lesson/what do you have to do – a week before, the day before, and what should you check on the day?
- If the pupils have to wait outside the room for another class to leave, what is your role as the class enters?
- How will you begin the lesson?
- What will you do if the class is slow to settle?
- Are there any rules you want to establish from the beginning?
- How do you set about establishing a good working relationship with the class?
- How will you finish the lesson?
- What are your plans for the other six or seven lessons that you will have to teach that day?

To find the answers to these questions read on ...

CHAPTER 2

Adjusting to the job

CASE STUDY 2.1. FOR REFLECTION

It was much harder than I expected

I thought I knew what it would be like because on teaching practice we were in school 70 per cent of the time, but it was actually quite different in a lot of respects, and in the first term I started work it was very much harder than I expected. Other staff laughed and said my timetable was lighter than theirs because I was an NQT, but it didn't feel light. I suppose it was that I had to teach a lot more than on teaching practice, when some of the time was spent on observing or other activities.

Now I know what it is like to go from Tuesday morning 'til Thursday afternoon without a free period. Then three of my free periods came together and I found it difficult to use them effectively because I needed a break so badly, and anyway I had to spend one of them with my head of department. That session was helpful except that I felt a bit like the pupils – I had to have my homework up to date, or a really good excuse, or she would think I couldn't cope.

I hadn't realized how much preparation there would be. The pupils are quite bright and I have a lot of exam classes. I found that we got through everything that I had prepared in much less time than it took me to prepare it, and as for the marking – it was endless. I never seemed to be without at least one set of books. I had got married in the summer after I qualified. My husband isn't a teacher. He commutes into town every day and I drive out of town to work. The journey takes me quite a while. I go to work early to miss the traffic, but it is hard to avoid it on the journey home, so sometimes I am in after John and dinner isn't ready. He's quite good about helping out, but much less sympathetic about all the work that I bring home. He says he can understand my having to do preparation or marking once a week, but surely it shouldn't be necessary for me to have to work every night, but I can't get it all done at school. He has begun to get irritated every time I pick up a pile of books to mark and the rows increase my tiredness, which added to my problems, because on the occasions when I yielded to his persuasion not to work, I felt guilty about it and anyway was so shattered that he said I was no fun to be with . . . .

A new job, newly wed at the same time, a difficult journey to and from work, a heavy load of lesson preparation and marking, forging relationships with pupils and colleagues, and fitting into the department team have all put this new teacher under pressure, so it was not surprising that she has found adjusting to the job a shattering experience.

Adjusting to Work

The woman in this case study found being an NQT very different from being a student on teaching practice. This is probably the first adjustment you will have to make, so what are the key differences from being a student?

■ You can no longer look to the college for support – you are a qualified practitioner now.
■ There won't be a group of students facing the same problems as you.
■ You may be the only NQT on the staff.
■ You may be on a short-term contract facing pressure to succeed.
■ The pupils' expectations of you will be higher – you are a real teacher now.
■ You will not be able to move on to another practice somewhere else next term, so you can't afford mistakes.
■ The previous factors may make you more cautious about experimenting in the classroom.
■ You have a job description, defined responsibilities and a full role in the department team.
■ You have to work a full timetable and cope with time and institutional pressure.

A typical day – NQT description:

Getting into school at 7.30 am.

Leaving at 5.30 pm.
Doing two to three hours preparation or marking at home.
Collapsing.

This description echoes the one given in the case study. Both of these teachers are finding making the adjustment from being a student to being a qualified teacher difficult. Experienced teachers would support this perception of the changeover:

> It's a kind of rite of passage; you are moving from a fairly protected environment into the world. There's no tutor, although nowadays you may have a mentor. It is not at all the same as being in college with your peer group.

Teaching is a very demanding profession and it would be wrong to expect the first few months in the job to be plain sailing. Just how difficult you find it will depend on a number of factors, eg:

- volume of work
- type and difficulty of the school
- academic or other pressures
- friendliness or otherwise of the staff and pupils.

Most of all, it will depend on your own attitude and approach. The teacher in the case study allowed herself to be overwhelmed by all the demands upon her time. In order to help you avoid her fate we need to find some answers to the question, 'What could she have done to make that first term easier to cope with?'

The first thing this teacher should do is to review her own self management, because part of the answer lies in effective use of time. It is a common mistake on the part of an NQT to try to be a perfectionist. Obviously you will want to do things as well as possible, but you need to be realistic about what you can manage and to decide what your priorities are.

This teacher is obviously spending a great deal of time on preparing lessons and marking pupils' work. What is more, she is having to do almost all of it at home in the evenings when she is already tired and to the increasing irritation of her husband. She is probably trying to mark too much, so her first decision has to be about how much marking she can do in the time available each week (the issue of marking is addressed later in this book). Discussion with her head of department (HOD) could establish some ground rules for marking. She could also look for ways in which she could do more of it in school. Her description of her first term indicated that she arrived early because of the traffic problems, but not how she used that time once at school. This patch of time could be very useful – the school will be at its quietest, few pupils will be around to knock on the staffroom door and she could get on with work relatively undisturbed. This could be the time to dispose of a set of marking as she is at her freshest. We have suggested one solution for this NQT; what should you do if you are faced with this kind of problem? Start by trying to stand back from the problem and work out when you can allocate a spot of regular time for marking, make it dedicated time and stick to it. Time management is dealt with more fully in Chapter 10, on keeping sane.

The case study also suggests that the teacher is trying to manage entirely on her own. Her HOD is spending time with her each week, but the NQT seems to consider this as adding to her burdens and to regard it as having her homework checked. This may reflect on the character and leadership style of this particular HOD, but it is a pity, because when you are feeling unsure of yourself in those first traumatic weeks, it is important to know that there are people on the teaching staff whose job descriptions include responsibility for helping you. Of course some will do it more willingly and better than others, but since part of their higher salary is being earned by taking managerial responsibility for other members of staff, they should be monitoring your progress and supplying you with the help and support that you need. So who has responsibility for you and what kind of support can you expect to get?

Support Structures – Mentors

Who is Responsible for You?

Your immediate line manager is your HOD, who should be your main source of information and help, especially as regards your subject teaching. A good HOD should guide your steps smoothly through the hazards of your first year's teaching.

One of the problems of school management structures is that people find that they have more than one manager. For example, if you are in a large department or faculty there may be a head of faculty with overall responsibility for the faculty staff, but there are also HODs for each of the subjects within the faculty, and you could become the object of a tug-of-war or, more likely, neglected by both your possible managers. Similarly, if you teach in more than one subject area, eg, English and religious studies, geography and history, you may find yourself with divided loyalties. If you have a form or tutor group you will also have a pastoral manager, the year head or head of house, who should brief you about what to do at registration and in form time, provide guidance about how to deliver the PSHE programme and support you if problems arise with any member of the group. Having too many managers can be confusing and it creates potentially conflicting demands and standards, but access to more than one manager can give you a lot of possible support, so try to turn this into an advantage. For a start it will mean that you do not have to go to the same person too frequently and it gives you a choice, especially if one of your managers turns out to be not terribly sympathetic to your problems.

What Kind of Support do NQTs Receive?

In a good school your various managers will have given thought to what areas of responsibility each will take in regard to you and how often each of them will see you. In a poorly managed school this will be much more haphazard and you may get very little support.

CASE STUDY 2.2. FOR REFLECTION

The list below is taken from the DES Education Project, 1976–81 (Kerry, 1982) and summarizes the kind of help the teachers participating in the project received during their first year of teaching:

- a general invitation to discuss problems with someone in authority ('My door is always open...')
- NQT meetings in school and/or area bases
- guidance on syllabus matters from the HOD or departmental staff.
- support on disciplinary matters from pastoral staff
- information about school customs and procedures
- sheltered timetable, lower allocation of difficult classes
- light timetable for the first year
- release for Inservice courses
- cooperative planning with other staff in team-teaching
- opportunities to watch other staff and other departments at work.

Although this list was compiled some years ago, any survey undertaken in schools today is likely to produce similar results. So what does this list tell us? It indicates a variety of uncoordinated provision from a number of different sources and that several people may have responsibility for supporting you. For this reason many NQTs came to feel that they needed a more formal programme of support. When asked what they wanted from such a system, a group of NQTs suggested that time should be set aside each week for:

- dealing with important issues as they arise
- joint planning of work
- advice on methods and resources
- shared teaching and mutual observation
- feedback on effectiveness – constructive evaluation.

How should schools set about providing a framework which will help NQTs address the problems that they encounter as these emerge, and which would give them a clear and logical insight into how experienced teachers approached these problems and issues? The role of professional tutor has begun to develop in schools to address this need. What this means is that the school has nominated a senior member of staff, usually but not exclusively a senior teacher or deputy head, who has overall responsibility for staff development and for managing the induction of all new teachers and coordinating the support they receive. The role of a professional tutor, however, is a coordinating one; the main agent in providing support for a new teacher is the teacher-tutor or mentor.

What Does a Mentor Do?

What does the term mentoring mean? Basically it means that an experienced member of staff will provide support for an inexperienced member of staff or one undertaking a new role, while the teacher grows into the job. The mentor may be your HOD, but quite often it is someone with three or four years' experience in the post, who hasn't so many other responsibilities that s/he hasn't time to listen to your problems, and who can relate to you and understand the difficulties that you are experiencing. In some schools this person is called the teacher-tutor; more commonly nowadays s/he is called a mentor.

Working with an experienced teacher enables the new teacher

to learn on the job. Ideally, the mentor should enhance the new teacher's experience by providing:

- the challenge which stretches the new teacher, encourages him/her to analyse what s/he has learnt from the experience and to work out a set of educational values
- the sponsorship which helps create a network, through making introductions, or suggesting meetings or courses which it would be useful for the new teacher to attend
- the support which protects and sustains the teacher when difficulties are experienced
- the praise and encouragement which helps the new teacher build up his/her esteem.

In this way the NQT grows into the profession and successfully manages the difficult transition from new teacher to valued colleague. How this could work is illustrated in Figures 2.1 and 2.2. (I am indebted for the mentoring diagrams to the Education Department of Oxford Brookes University.) The view of mentoring shown in the figures is of the mentor as a catalyst and the mentoring cycle as central to the support of the new teacher.

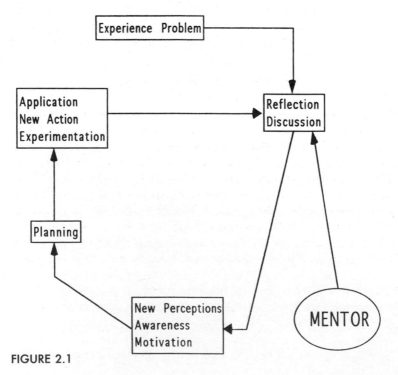

FIGURE 2.1

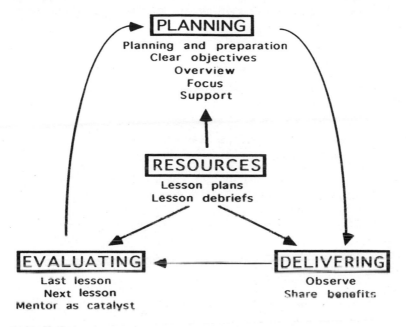

FIGURE 2.2

CASE STUDY 2.3. FOR REFLECTION

A Mentoring Programme

The programme below shows how a mentor could support the new teacher over the first year in a school. It is taken from the Teacher Education Project coordinated by Professor Ted Wragg and Dr Clive Sutton, which examined in-school provision for student teachers and NQTs (see Kerry, 1982). It is a role specification, spelling out what is expected of the mentor, and provides a checklist of responsibilities. It was designed to help the mentor reflect on his/her role but it is also useful for you as an NQT because it can serve as a guide to the kind of help a good mentor could provide for you. Notice that it is divided into three phases: before term starts, the first term and the first year.

Before the NQT takes up his/her post:
In the months between college and employment the mentor should:

■   contact the NQT giving him/her an explanation of the mentor role

- inform him/her about any activities for NQTs which take place early in the school year
- offer guidance with general school problems which may arise when the NQT has visited the school, collected his/her timetable, etc.
- arrange to meet him/her on his preliminary visit to the school
- provide him/her with appropriate maps, staff lists, copy of the school handbook, etc.

When the NQT first arrives in September the mentor should:

- bring to his/her attention the range of matters relating to professional societies (unions, subject groups, etc.)
- go over conditions of service, salaries, sickness procedures, etc.
- introduce him/her to resources and facilities
- explain the social workings of the school including those related to the staff room, staff meetings, administrative procedures, contacts with parents
- interpret school policies and procedures for such things as homework, booking equipment, disciplinary sanctions, staff duties, visits, assembly and reports
- sponsor him/her and help him/her make initial contacts with, for example, the head and deputies; heads of faculty; heads of year or house; caretaker; site manager; ancillary staff; careers, welfare and psychological service staff
- anticipate any specific teaching problems s/he may have, eg, with unfamiliar forms of organization such as team teaching, mixed ability groups, resource-based/flexible learning, etc.
- sift out any pupils with extraordinary problems which the NQT should know about immediately, eg, the pupil prone to mild fits or asthma.

During the first year the mentor should support the NQT by:

- encouraging the NQT to take part in team-teaching activities
- observing him/her at work in the classroom
- discussing the observations, offering constructive criticisms and help towards improving skills
- conducting seminars for all the school's NQTs to pool problems and ideas
- helping to solve administrative or timetable problems
- referring complex problems to the appropriate member of staff
- informing the NQT about his/her progress in class management and control, teaching skills, preparation, handling of pupils, etc.

- liaising with senior staff about the progress of the NQT and necessary action
- feeding back to the NQT
- arranging Inset opportunities for the NQT
- integrating the NQT into the extra-curricular life of the school
- arranging external assessment as necessary
- reviewing the NQT's progress at the end of the year.

The short case studies which follow illustrate some situations in which a mentoring system could help a new teacher.

CASE STUDIES 2.4–2.6. FOR ACTION/DISCUSSION

Case study 2.4.

My head of department seemed charming and kept telling me how she really wanted to help me. She remembered what it had been like to be a new teacher and wanted to give me all the support she could, but she never seemed to get round to doing anything. It's a small department, only the two of us, so there is no one else I can consult. I gave her my lesson plans and she said they looked 'OK', but I don't think she ever read them. She keeps saying how important it is to talk over how to approach the next core unit for KS 3 before we start it, but of course we haven't. She talks about my coming to see her teach, which I would like very much, but nothing has come of it. Needless to say she hasn't been to see me teach. She keeps meaning to find the department assessment scheme for me and I need it urgently. I wonder if she knows where it is? Sometimes I wonder if it exists at all. There is a parents' evening for Year 11 shortly. It is my first one and I am not sure what things to say to the parents. I have asked my head of department, but ....

Case study 2.5.

He's the real old-style head of department. I have to submit all my lesson plans, show my mark schemes, give in a set of books once a fortnight so that he can see that I am up-to-date and that I've followed his approved scheme and he regularly inspects my lessons, and then I am summoned to see how much better he does it. I wouldn't mind so much but whatever I do – it's no good. He picks holes in absolutely everything and I have come to dread those weekly sessions with him. What makes it worse is that, although he doesn't say anything in front of the pupils, his attitude is clear and they guess and it affects their behaviour. Can I really be that bad?

Case study 2.6

When I first came she was all over me and spent so much time going through work with me that I found it quite oppressive, but when I began to experience problems, my head of department dropped me like a hot cake. Some of the problems were health-related and I was absent from school quite a bit, which made me feel very vulnerable about my position. It was then that I could have done with some help, but she treated me like a pariah. I think she thought I was deliberately letting down the department.

For action:
In each of the case studies:

Analyse the issues involved in the case study.
How could a mentor help in this situation?
What advice would you give the NQT?

For discussion:

How could a mentor have helped the teacher in case study 2.4?

Strengths and Weaknesses of the System

Having a mentor available to provide guidance and support is a facility that should greatly benefit NQTs, and the use of mentoring in schools is increasing. How well is it working in practice and how have the NQTs reacted to it?

CASE STUDY 2.7. FOR REFLECTION

When a group of NQTs were asked recently what they valued in the mentoring system, they stressed:

- the opportunity to discuss problems with a critical friend
- the opportunity to see how another teacher worked
- sharing – ie, when the mentor shared problems s/he had faced as a new teacher

- encouragement at difficult times
- encouragement to try something new or difficult
- praise for new ideas or successful strategies, which in turn boosted confidence.

They also stressed how the relationship with the mentor changed and developed over the year. Early in the year, improving technical skills was very important, but with the passing of time, the developing relationship with a good mentor was increasingly valued for itself. Indeed the extent to which good mentoring was valued was summed up by one teacher who said, 'What I found I valued most was that I gained a real friend who helped and encouraged me.'

CASE STUDY 2.8. FOR DISCUSSION

A group of NQTs recently highlighted some things they found difficulty with during the first few terms:

- lack of self-confidence/shyness
- difficult conditions of work, eg, workload or problems within the department
- wanting to seek advice but not knowing who from, how or what messages it might give
- working as part of a departmental team
- supporting and carrying out the general rules of the school
- unacceptable advice/reluctance to accept it
- lack of knowledge about the children's backgrounds
- fatigue – leading to inability to attend courses or take on extra-curricular activities
- logistical problems, eg, transport, which led to difficulties in attending courses or functions
- communication problems – 'Nobody told me what was going on.'

For discussion:

How could a mentor help new teachers with these problems?

Not all NQTs found the experience rewarding or supportive. Like any other system, mentoring can have its problems. Those most commonly experienced include:

- no clear demarcation between the responsibility of the mentor and the subject HOD – 'I didn't know which of them I was expected to consult about my problems'

- insufficient time – 'It seemed a good idea in theory but in practice we never had enough time'
- mismatch between the needs of the NQT and the expertise of the mentor – 'I can't think why they chose him – he's so good himself that I find it demoralizing and he gets so impatient with me ...'
- too judgemental – 'It felt like having two HODs instead of one ...' or, 'I thought it was a version of big brotherism ...'
- lack of power – 'My mentor sympathized, but didn't seem to be able to do anything for me ...'

The case studies above illustrate clearly that in practice the mentoring system can be rather hit-or-miss. This is because it depends for its credibility on:

- the quality of the mentor – thus the choice is crucial
- the provision of a clear role specification – so that both sides understand what a mentor can be expected to do
- the mentor having the power to put things right – or access to someone who does!

The system has enormous potential, so if it is available in your school, try to make it work for you.

Adjusting to the Department – Working in a Team

As well as adjusting to the working environment, you have to adjust to the department. You have to learn how it works and how to fit into the departmental team. When you join the school, you become a member of a number of teams – department, faculty, cross-curricular, year/house, etc. – all of which make demands upon you. Of these, the department team is probably the one which is most important to you and in this section we shall concentrate on fitting into the department, although the ideas suggested here are generally relevant and hopefully you will be able to adapt them to fit your needs.

CASE STUDY 2.9. FOR ACTION/DISCUSSION

At college they encouraged me to experiment and to use a variety of different teaching techniques, but this doesn't seem to be going down very well with some members of my department. Bill and

Jane say that it is very important that we all take the same approach to topics, and I've heard that, behind my back, they say that I'm a 'lefty trendy' and that my methods are unsound. I don't think that I am a 'lefty trendy' at all. But I think they are too set in their ways and I'm not sure that they really stretch the children ...' (New teacher talking to a friend.)

For action/discussion:

Analyse the issues involved in this case study.
How could a mentor help the NQT in this situation?
What advice would you give the new teacher?

This case study, where the new teacher was clearly finding difficulty fitting into an established department, illustrates one of the problems which might arise. Here are some other examples:

■ 'We don't do it that way' - conflict between what you have been taught at college and the methods used by the department
■ not accepted by the team   the new teacher becomes the 'odd man out'
■ problems arising from your prior experience, eg in industry – the department regard you as not being open to new ideas or working methods – have you become inflexible?
■ new broomism/know-it-all approach – goes down badly with the department
■ the issue of how much independence you can legitimately expect in the current educational climate and as a member of a departmental team.

There is a lot of advice available about how to lead a team, but very little has been written about becoming an effective member of a team, so how should you go about it?

Some Hints on How to Fit into the Departmental Team

Apply what you learnt at college
At college you will probably have learnt some theory about teams, the stages in their development and how they operate. If so, you will be able to draw upon your studies to gain an insight into the working of your new department. Being able to recognize the stage of development that the team is in, or what kind of a team it is, gets you started because you can then work

out what strategies you need to employ to help you relate to the team members and integrate successfully into the team.

If you haven't had the opportunity to learn about teams, a very useful introductory booklet is the Industrial Society's *Teamwork in Schools* (Trethowan, 1985). It gives you a clear definition of what a team is and takes you through the various stages in team development. The short description given below is included to provide you with a short cut, ie it is a basic guideline to how teams work.

CASE STUDY 2.10. FOR REFLECTION

A Checklist for Understanding Teams

1. What is a Team?

A team is a group of people who work or relate in a way which helps them achieve their common objective. In an effective team, team spirit has to be created so that the members work for the benefit of the group. To achieve its task, the group needs each member, and it is in the interest of the group to develop the skills of each member. Back biting and gossip causes team members to hold back on their performance and the task is not achieved. Good individuals do not automatically make good team members until they lean to operate as one. (Trethowan, 1985.)

2. Stages in Team Formation

There are four recognizable stages in team formation:

Forming – the initial stage when a team is put together; it is marked by formality and politeness.
Storming – the stage when tensions come out into the open, team members jockey for position and the leader has to establish his/her authority.
Norming – the welding stage, when the team begins to come together, tensions decrease and members take on more responsibilities.
Performing – the team reaches its target and becomes fully operational and effective. At this stage there is a high level of trust and confidence.

3. An Effective Team

- Shares agreed goals and common objectives.
- Clearly establishes its members' roles and has clear procedures.
- Establishes open lines of communication.
- Has a climate of mutual respect, support and trust.
- Confronts and resolves issues that cause conflict.
- Recognizes and values each person's contribution.
- Has appropriate and effective leadership.
- Develops its members as well as the team.
- Reviews its progress regularly.

4. Watch How it Works and Analyse the State of the Team

You will want to know how long the various members of the department have been in the team and what state of evolution it has reached. These factors will influence how the department reacts to a new member. If several of the team are fairly new themselves, they are unlikely to resent another newcomer, although if they are in the middle of the storming stage, you may find the experience rather traumatic! If the team is well established, it may have the confidence to welcome new blood, but it could be operating 'club culture' and close its ranks against you. It could feel threatened, particularly if it has become set in its ways, and you will have to be careful not to allow yourself to become the odd one out. If you find that this is the case, you will have to tread very carefully.

5. What is its Dominant Style?

Does the team do what it is told by its authoritarian leader or does it operate democratically? Watching how the department interrelates will tell you a lot about both the leader and the members. You will also learn a lot about how decisions are taken. When you have identified the dominant style, give some thought to whether your own approach fits in easily or not.

6. How Does the Team Communicate?

Frequently or rarely, through formal business mechanisms such as memos or over coffee or lunch? Notice what kind of things are discussed by the team and how fully. Is it only the minutiae of daily business? If a lot of the discussion is over coffee and sandwiches, does it mean that you should sit mainly with your department, as otherwise you will lose out on information or fail to build up a relationship with the other members?

7. What is the Dominant Relationship Pattern amongst the Members?

Is the team like an exclusive club or a loose association of members? How much real collaboration is there in preparing materials? Do the members support each other? Are the relationships warm and friendly or are the members cold and distant towards each other? Is it friendly on the surface but knife-in-the-back behind the scenes? How frequently do members visit each other's teaching rooms and for what purpose? Is it an effective team which fits The Industrial Society's description, or is it simply a group of ill-assorted individuals who happen to teach the same subject?

8. Find out What You are Expected to Contribute to the Team

When you join a team you can become an effective team member faster and more painlessly if you give some thought to what your special contribution could be. You may be the person with lots of ideas to offer; you may be a methodical planner, good at working out examination arrangements or organizing visits; you may particularly enjoy curriculum development, or be a whiz at handling visual aids or the new developments in computer technology, or you may be skilled in getting the department to reconcile differences. When you were appointed, did they choose you because you complement the skills and qualities of other members of the team or because they were looking for someone in their own image? Was the HOD looking for an infusion of ideas or simply for someone who will undertake a lot of the donkey work? You may not know the answer to these questions and you should also bear in mind that people take on different roles in different teams according to the mix of personalities and the demands of a particular situation.

Team Teaching

Having to participate in team teaching or sharing a class with a colleague or student teacher can be an unnerving experience for a new teacher, as case study 2.11 indicates. It is somehow much more threatening than sharing a class when you were a student, because subconsciously you feel that you have to prove yourself in a way that you did not have to when you were on teaching practice.

CASE STUDY 2.11. FOR ACTION

I had had to work at establishing a relationship with my year 10 class, then a student, Robin, came and he was attached to my year 10 group for two of their lessons so that he could compare them to a parallel set where he was working with the HOD. I was a little apprehensive because the HOD is such a good teacher. I feared that the student would think I was pathetic by comparison, but that turned out to be the least of my problems. Robin is extremely confident and the class took to him at once.

We teach through the medium of a foreign language and I always write the date on the board in that language. There is more than one correct way of doing this and Robin used a different version from the one I normally use. The pupils tend to think in terms of right or wrong and I saw them looking at me as if to say, 'He's doing it right, you were teaching us incorrectly.'

For action:

What problems does this NQT face?
How can a mentor help this NQT?
What advice would you give this NQT?

CHAPTER 3

The Logistics of Classroom Life

Planning and Preparation

'If I had planned it properly, it might have been different ... ' (NQT).

This NQT had learnt the hard way how crucial it is to the success of a lesson to plan and prepare it properly. When you are a student or an NQT, you will probably need to make very clear lesson plans, not just because your tutor or mentor wishes to see it, but because it is helpful for you to have a full plan and to build up a file of these to refer to when you need an idea or an approach. Later on, the mechanics of lesson preparation will be so familiar to you that you may not need a written lesson pro forma, or you will use very brief notes, but this does not mean that you will not go through the planning process. Your planning pro forma is not the same as your lesson notes, which contain the content of the lesson. Don't expect, even when you are very experienced, to be able to remember all the data that you will use in a series of lessons on a particular topic. An exemplar of the planning pro forma is given in case study 3.1.

CASE STUDY 3.1. EXEMPLAR, FOR REFLECTION.
A LESSON PLANNING PRO FORMA

Lesson plan   *Class/group*   *Date*

Title

Aims   *
            *
            *
            *

Context/place in sequence

Content and method

Beginning of lesson

Main development

Extension activities

Ending the lesson

Resources needed

Risk assessment

Homework set

Notes

There are five elements to good lesson preparation:

- deciding your objectives
- determining the content
- deciding the method of delivery
- preparing your resources
- working out the assessment method.

Deciding Your Objectives

You should start by deciding what you want to achieve from the lesson; this is different from deciding its content. Suppose that you are a history teacher delivering a component of Key Stage 3 about the seventeenth century. Your content would be about the events in the 1630s leading up to the Civil War in England, but what you really want from the lesson or series of lessons, is for the pupils to understand why there was a Civil War. Your lesson/s are about historical understanding and particularly about causation. Your objective would be for the pupils to understand long- and short-term causes in the context of the Civil War. You may find that you have more than one objective, and if so, you will need to decide whether all the objectives are as important as each other, and to think through whether you are actually able to deliver more than one objective in a lesson, especially when you are new to the job. Being clear about what you want to achieve is very important to your success.

CASE STUDY 3.2. FOR ACTION/REFLECTION

If you want to use this case study for group discussion, use the discussion points before reading the 'for reflection' section which analyses the case study.

**Lesson objectives: subject matter mathematics
– perimeters**

1. To ensure that the Y8 class understand how perimeters are determined.
2. To encourage pupils to participate actively.
3. To encourage pupils to work together effectively.
4. To contribute to the department project on barriers.

Richard's lesson was to be observed by the HOD so he prepared it carefully. He began by reinforcing previous knowledge which the class would have to use to understand and to cope with the new topic. To do this, he asked questions and pupils put up their hands to answer. Quite a lot of hands went up each time he asked a question, and Richard made sure that he accepted answers from a variety of pupils. On several occasions, however, there were three or four incorrect guesses before the right answer was given. Richard was patient and persevered, encouraging the pupils, who finally offered the correct answer. This took about ten minutes, until finally he was able to move on to the new work, establishing through whole-class teaching, and by drawing diagrams on the white board, the method of working out perimeters. Again he used question and answer, backing the answers with some additional explanation.

Richard's HOD, Ian, noticed that a number of pupils seemed very willing to give answers, even if these were incorrect. Other pupils made little contribution to the lesson, and it was difficult to tell their level of involvement. Ian moved his seat so that he could see more of the class. There was no obvious inattention. The occasional child seemed to be doodling, but most were listening. Occasionally Richard selected a pupil who had not put up his/her hand and this produced about the same ratio of correct to incorrect answers as asking the more willing pupils. All the drawing on the white board was done by Richard.

About halfway through the double period, Richard set the pupils to work out for themselves some examples of perimeters. To do this work they sat, as they had for the lesson, in groups of about six around tables. There was a hum of conversation and activity. Arun and Atul were heard quietly discussing the latest cricket score; Michelle and Anna's conversation seemed to be about what they would do at the weekend. Donovan was clearly day-dreaming and Richard had to speak to him sharply to recover his attention but, when eventually Donovan had worked out a correct example, Richard praised him for his effort. Richard made his way around the tables, helping the pupils individually and had got round most of the tables by the time that the bell went to end the lesson. Homework was to complete the examples. The class left chatting cheerfully; now it was time for Richard and Ian to talk.

For action/discussion:

Analyse the lesson to see how far it met each of its objectives. How would you approach discussing this lesson with Richard? What advice would you give Richard and on what grounds? Draw up an action plan for Richard.

For reflection:
Richard had set himself four objectives for this lesson. They are simply numbered 1–4, so we can not tell whether they are in order of importance or not. Achieving four objectives in one lesson is difficult even for an experienced teacher, so Richard had set himself a hard task. Let us now examine to what extent he had met them.

Richard's first objective was to ensure that the pupils understood how to work out perimeters. He worked hard during the lesson to get the pupils to understand and was prepared to persevere at each stage. It would seem from the answers given and the written work done in class, that for the majority of the pupils in the group he had achieved his objective, and judged by this criterion, it was a satisfactory/successful lesson.

He also made some attempt to achieve his second objective – to get the pupils to participate – but here his methods to some extent defeated his end. A range of pupils answered questions orally, some very willingly. Richard tried to involve more pupils by asking some who had not volunteered, but participation for about half of this double lesson was through question and answer on closed questions – an answer was either right or wrong. He tried to encourage pupils by praising correct answers, but the protracted struggle to get the right answer affected the pace and momentum of the lesson. (Advice on questioning techniques can be found in Chapter 6.)

Only Richard wrote on the board – coming out to the front to work out an example could have involved pupils in a different way from simply answering questions. During the second half of the lesson when the pupils were working out examples, Richard made his way round the tables, so that virtually every child received some individual attention, but it was difficult for him to ensure that they were all working actively all the time. A few pupils were clearly off-task, or preoccupied with other things. As he went round the room, Richard picked up on this; for example, he focused Donovan's attention back onto the work in hand and got him to finish an example. But, although most pupils did concentrate and did the work set, this hardly meets the objective of active participation. There was not the real excitement about this group of pupils at work which would have occurred with active participation from them all.

The third objective was to encourage pupils to work together effectively, but there was no sign that they were working together at all, either in pairs or in groups of sixes; rather the pupils seemed to be doing individual work on the examples set. Any conversation was social, not mathematical. No one even seemed to be comparing his/her results with those of another pupil. Working in pairs could have actually helped Richard to achieve his first and second objectives, because explaining to each other is an effective teaching technique. Not only could it have helped understanding, but it could also have raised the level of involvement. Groups could have been set different examples, or could have competed to see who could do the most examples, perhaps with a class certificate for the group who did best.

It is difficult to know how this lesson was meant to contribute to the department project on barriers, as this was not mentioned by anyone at any stage of the lesson. Possibly in his anxiety at having his HOD present, Richard forgot it, but there is no indication at all that this was meant to be anything other than a lesson on perimeters. Making it relevant to a cross-curricular project could actually have generated a greater level of pupil involvement in what they must have seen as a very pedestrian lesson. If this skill is to be used towards a larger project, it needs to be flagged at this stage, not simply because it would maintain the pupils' interest, but so that they understood what would be expected of them.

Richard would seem to have met only one of his four objectives. Was this because he set himself too many objectives, or because they were incompatible? The answer probably is neither. He might have been aiming high, but the four objectives were certainly not incompatible. Achieving the last two objectives would actually have helped Richard achieve the first two. His problem seems to have been that he only really thought about his first priority – getting the pupils to understand – and to have tagged the other objectives onto the list, perhaps in the hope of impressing his HOD.

Advising Richard

How should Ian, as Richard's HOD, approach the issue that Richard has largely failed to meet his objectives? The usual way into a discussion with a colleague about how s/he has performed, is to find out what the teacher's own perception of the lesson is. Ian would probably start, therefore, by asking Richard what things he thought went well and what he thought might need further work. This would give Ian the opportunity to praise good features of the lesson, such as the way that Richard encouraged and drew in pupils, but it would also, if Ian were skilful enough, get Richard to raise some of the difficulties himself. This could lead them on to discuss the objectives set, why Richard had chosen them and how appropriate they were.

However sensitively Ian dealt with it, it needed to be faced that perhaps Richard was trying to run before he could walk. There were not necessarily too many objectives, though meeting four at one time sets a teacher a hard task, but Richard clearly needed to give more thought to the objectives he set. He had to decide whether they were all equally important and to work out how he proposed to achieve them. Being clear about what you want to achieve in a lesson or series of lessons means that you have to think very carefully indeed about your objectives to make sure that they are appropriate and to work out what you will have to do in order to carry them out. Ian would also need to stress how important it is that the objectives are shared with and understood by the pupils. In this lesson the pupils would have grasped only that they were being taught how to work out perimeters.

For reflection:
Setting and meeting objectives can be difficult for a new teacher. The case study above offered some suggestions about how a Head of Department could work through this kind of problem with an NQT. What approach is adopted in your own school and how does it compare with the suggestions offered? What strategy do you think Ian should adopt in order to help Richard improve his performance?

Determining the Content

Think of a lesson both as a coherent whole and as a package of learning activities. (Kyriacou, 1991.)

Once you have decided your learning objectives, the next question is, 'How are you going to get there?' This question centres on lesson content and the learning activities through which you will deliver the topic. Although much of the content is now determined by the National Curriculum, there is still a lot of scope for individual decision making. In some areas of the curriculum there is a menu of options from which your department will make choices and you should get the opportunity to contribute to that choice. How you teach the topics and what learning activities you employ are still largely a matter of departmental or individual decision, so what factors do you have to take into account when deciding how to teach a lesson?

The Context

Is it a one-off lesson or part of a series? If it is part of a larger topic, how sequential will your content or activities need to be?

Being part of a series will affect the range of activities you use and how often you vary them. How much time you can spend on a topic will influence you in determining how superficially or thoroughly you will be able to cover it. The timing of a lesson, ie whether it is early or late in the week, a single or double lesson, or most of all whether it is the last period on Friday afternoon will also affect your content and method of delivery.

The Shape of a Lesson

In your planning it would be helpful to think about how the time should be organized. A lesson should have a clear structure. It normally divides into three phases or sections:

- beginning section – usually teacher led, sets the context/scene
- middle section – longest section, contains the major learning experience, varied activities
- final section – summarize what has been learnt, recall, reinforce, assess progress, relate or generally comment on the lesson.

This structure could generally act as a 'template' around which you plan the activities.

The Teaching Group

How do you best meet the needs of the group? You have to take into account their abilities, interests and motivation. Is your audience a set, a stream or a mixed ability group? Think about the teaching group and how it is likely to respond to the activities that you are planning. As you get to know a group of children, you will begin to learn what works well with them. Do they respond best to whole-class teaching? Do you have a collection of individuals who really dislike group/team work? How do they respond to timed activities? How often should you make them use a format that they don't much like?

Does it Contribute to a Wider Objective?

In case study 3.2, the lesson on how you worked out a perimeter was meant to contribute to a project, but unless some pupils were very good at making links, they would not have known. At some stage of the lesson, it should have been clearly stated that the technique that was being taught could be used in the department barriers project. You may have to make a contribution to one or more of the cross-curricular themes, so when you begin to think about how you will deliver a particular topic, take cross-curricular issues into account and decide when you will flag up economic awareness or whichever theme is appropriate. In history for example, the French Revolution, currently an optional module in KS3, helps to deliver both economic awareness because of the economic factors which helped to bring about the Revolution, and citizenship/political awareness because of the dissatisfaction with the existing regime and the desire for democracy.

What Forms of Activity Best Deliver the Skills or Techniques You have to Teach?

There is usually more than one way that you can teach a particular topic so you should think about what approach will work best in terms of the topic itself. How much of the lesson will be class teaching? How much information should you give? What form of exercise will best allow them to try to use the new skill or technique? Remember that children often learn more from explaining to each other than from listening to you, and think about how you can use this factor.

How do You Stretch/Stimulate the Pupils?

This links to deciding your objectives. It is essential that not only is your lesson matched to the abilities of the pupils with appropriate activities, but also that it is stimulating and makes demands on them intellectually, and in a way that provides a positive experience. In the mathematics lesson, in case study 3.2, the children went along with it cooperatively, but it was not clear how far it stretched all of them; there was no attempt at differentiation and they were not excited by the lesson. Providing the right level of stimulus is not an easy task, so your planning must take account of how you will tackle it. You will also need to work out when during the lesson you should vary the activities in order to keep the stimulus going.

Your own Expertise/Whether to Play Safe

It is tempting, particularly when you are very busy or tired, to stick to the kind of activities that you know will go well or which do not involve you in too much preparation. Planning over a long period of time helps you think ahead about what you will need to do and when it should be done, so that if you want to try something difficult, you do so in the best possible conditions. It is also important to reflect on whether and when you should try again an activity which didn't go too well last time. At least you will learn whether the fault lay with you or the group. Practising techniques helps you to improve them.

Thinking through these issues at the planning stage can take a while and you may feel that you simply haven't got the time, but you can think about a lot of these points together rather than separately. Thorough planning and preparation do pay enormous dividends as you are much more likely to teach effectively if you have thought about how you are going to approach the task.

Deciding the Method of Delivery

Planning and Managing Different Types of Activities

A wide variety of learning activities can be employed to deliver your lesson, for example:

- you can set the whole class a task or an exercise which they work through individually
- you can hold a discussion or a debate
- you can get pupils to work in small groups or pairs
- you can use role play or simulation
- you may have to manage practical work.

Whatever the activity you have in mind, your starting point should always be to ask yourself two questions which will act as a check. They are:

1. Is it the best way to deliver this part of this lesson?
2. Have you organized it so that it will work?

Getting the answers to these two questions right can make all the difference to the success of your lesson and prevent the pupils from having a very frustrating experience, which in turn will affect your relationship with them and your class control!

For reflection:

Almost every task or activity can lead to chaos unless you give thought to the organisation of how and when the pupils are to do what is required of them. (Kyriacou, 1991.)

The section which follows is intended to provide a guide to planning and managing some of the possible lesson activities.

Classwork

In classwork the pupils work individually on the same task. This kind of session is frequently used to check the understanding of a topic by making the pupils do an exercise or assignment. It often follows on from a piece of teacher exposition and makes the pupils demonstrate that they have listened. It also tests whether they can apply their knowledge of what has been learned so far. It is the most commonly used teaching strategy and you are likely to use it a lot, so it is crucial that you do it well.

Some hints for managing classwork

Make sure that the task is appropriate and matches the ability level of the class.

Issue clear instructions at the start. You can do this orally, by writing on the board or by using a worksheet.

Settle the class down and make sure that everyone is working quietly. Reiterate the instruction about the noise level if necessary.

Monitor how well the activity is going by circulating round the room and having a quiet word with each pupil, checking his/her progress by asking the occasional question to probe how much the child has understood and what strategies s/he is adopting. You will also want to inspect the written work.

You could also use some of the time to see some pupils with their work, but if they bring it up to your table to discuss it, you must make sure that you scan the room regularly, otherwise the class may lose concentration and begin to chat.

Circulating round the room will enable you to get a good feel of how well the activity is working and if the pupils are experiencing difficulties.

Sometimes you will find that, in the light of what you have seen, you may want to halt the activity briefly and give additional instructions. Try not to do this too often. Case study 4.2 (page 81) illustrates how easy it is to interrupt the class's concentration and it may be difficult to settle the pupils again.

Your planning should include ideas for extension work for the more able pupils, who may finish the task well before time. Make sure that the additional work stretches the pupils and is not simply 'more of the same'.

It is usually a good idea to draw together the group at the end of the activity and make some general points or conclusions.

Managing Group Work

Case study 3.2 provided us with an example of a situation where group work was inappropriate. Let us look again at this section of the case study to see why this was so:

> Richard set the group to work out for themselves some examples of perimeters. To do this work, he sat them in groups of about six around tables. There was a hum of conversation and activity. Atul and Arun were heard quietly discussing the latest cricket score. Michelle and Anna's conversation seemed to be about what they should do at the weekend. Donovan was clearly day-dreaming, and Richard had to speak sharply to him to recover his attention ... Richard made his way around the tables, helping and encouraging the pupils individually and had got round most of the tables by the end of the lesson. Homework was to complete the examples....

■ The task was not tailored for group work – it was being done individually
■ There was no generation of ideas or collaborative learning.
■ Any conversation was purely social – about leisure time activities
■ Homework was also a task to be done individually – the pupils had to work out more examples.
■ The task could possibly have benefited from being done in pairs, so that the pupils could have helped each other, but it is not a good example of how to use group work, so when should you introduce group work into a lesson?

It is an extremely valuable tool for problem solving, generating ideas and working as a team. It is for when learning would benefit from a small number of pupils thinking collaboratively. An exemplar of a team task is given below:

CASE STUDY 3.3 EXEMPLAR OF A GROUP TASK

Christmas Bauble Exercise

Task Brief

Working as a team, design and make a container to hold three Christmas tree baubles. You are working to a time limit, and may use *only* the materials provided, some of which may be 'bought' using the 'money' provided. Your design must meet certain criteria:

1. It must protect the goods from accidental breakage.
2. It must be suitable for shop display purposes (ie, the goods will not need to be unpacked in order to display them).
3. It must look attractive – you don't want customers buying another brand of bauble.
4. It should be reasonably cost effective.

At the end of the afternoon your container will be tested to see to what extent it fulfils criterion number 1. Criteria numbers 2–4 will also be assessed.

The Test: Your container will be dropped from a height of 1 metre in order to see what kind of damage occurs. While this is going on you will also be given the chance to see the ideas that other teams have come up with.

For this part of the exercise you need to have produced:

1. A final version of your chosen idea.
2. A diagram to show how your container is constructed.
3. Your rough workings for *all* your preliminary ideas (whatever form this takes)
4. The final cost of your container.

You must display all of these together with any unused 'bought' materials.

Some hints for handling group work

Start with the objective you want to achieve and make sure that it is a suitable vehicle for group work.

Make sure that the seating arrangements facilitate group work. If the room is unsuitable, see if a room change is possible.

Think carefully about the size of the group. If in doubt, keep the groups small. Logistically, groups with more than four pupils will need more supervision than smaller groups.

You will have to think about who will be in the groups. The

composition of the group will affect its chances of success. You will have to base your decision about how to allocate pupils to groups on your knowledge of the class. Do friends work well with each other or are they better apart? Is the class still of an age where boys and girls won't mix and will resent being put together? Are there still some individuals who do not fit in and will have difficulty in being accepted into a group? What groupings of pupils will produce a good mix and productive teams?

Allocation of roles within a team can also be contentious, so give some thought to how far this is up to you to decide and what decisions should be made by the team. How directive you should be will depend on how well you know the class and whether they are used to this type of activity. It is likely that early in your relationship with the class, you will be more directive than later on. As the pupils become more confident and understand better what is involved, they will probably be able to take on more responsibility for defining and carrying out the task.

Monitoring and supervising group work sessions takes a lot of skill. You have to keep an eye on what all the groups are doing, see that groups get help when they need it and that no group has to wait about with nothing that they can do.

Make the necessary arrangements for feedback. Will they need to use a flip chart? Should the group appoint a scribe or reporter to act as spokesperson? Is there to be a plenary in which the threads are drawn together?

CASE STUDY 3.4. FOR ACTION

Every time we have to work in groups, I get left out, because no one asks me to be in his or her group. I feel very awkward and embarrassed. Last week I ended up having to work with the teacher and afterwards the others were laughing and joking about it. (An upset Y7 pupil has been sent to the year head for refusing to take part in group work.)

For action:
You are the class teacher – how could you manage the lesson to make it a more positive experience for this pupil?

CASE STUDY 3.5. FOR ACTION

You have divided your Year 12 A-level class into small groups of three or four and set them a problem. After the class Erica comes to see you. 'I can't do group work ,' she says. 'I can never think of anything to say and I just sit there feeling stupid.'

For action:

You are the teacher – what approach should you take in this situation?
How can you make group work a more positive experience for this student?

Managing Role Play or Simulations

The purpose of role play is to enhance the pupils' understanding by acting out a situation. It is most commonly used in arts subjects such as English or history, and will focus on a dramatic event or situation which the class or group will act out. For a new teacher, managing role play could be a minefield – a recipe for chaos.

CASE STUDY 3.6. FOR ACTION

I was pleased when Terry said that he would be doing a simulation. I see very few classes where the pupils are not seated at their desks or tables, and I was pleased with his initiative, but oh dear! They were dramatizing the story of Joan of Arc for some reason. There was plenty of space for them to act as Room 8 is probably the largest teaching space in the school, and it could have been very effective, but the size of the room seemed to have added to the problem because the pupils wandered about everywhere and the whole thing was a shambles. It was very difficult to tell what was going on. A few pupils had brought clothes to change into. I suspect this was a ploy to change out of their school uniform for the lesson. It certainly added to the confusion. Some pupils seemed to know what they were supposed to do, but most did not, and they kept arguing. I kept expecting Terry to do something about all this, but he didn't – he just let it happen. I think it had got away from him altogether. Finally one of the girls got really angry and shouted at them, and things quietened down a bit and we struggled through the last few scenes. I should have hated to have been teaching next door, or to be the teacher who had to use Room 8 after this class. No attempt was made to tidy up. (HOD discussing with a friend a lesson that he had observed recently.)

For discussion:

What mistakes had Terry made?
What does this case study indicate about the use of role play in lessons – suggest reasons.
What advice would you give Terry and on what grounds?
What advice would you give the HOD?

Some hints for handling simulations and role play

In this case study the observer was not clear why the story of Joan of Arc was being dramatized by the class. The first criterion for deciding to use a particular teaching technique must always be to ask yourself why you want to use this approach and to think whether it is the most suitable vehicle for the desired learning outcome. It is doubtful whether the class in the case study learned anything from this lesson.

Once you have decided that role play is appropriate, then, like any other classroom activity, you have to work to clear rules and procedures, which are known and accepted by everyone involved. For example: all noise must be purposeful. Role play must not be an excuse for rowdy behaviour, and you have to establish what the acceptable noise level should be. Those not involved in a particular scene must watch quietly.

Role play does not just happen – it needs a great deal of thought and preparation, perhaps more than for a more sedentary lesson. In the case study no one seems to be clear about what they should be doing: this indicated insufficient preparation prior to the lesson. Role play can be scripted or unscripted; either way the participants need some guidance. A briefing sheet for each participant, explaining who their character is and how the person is likely to behave, is a good way to help the pupils understand the characters and create their roles.

How you organize and use the space available will also contribute to the effectiveness of the lesson. Often the space is too small, and you have to work in cramped conditions. In the case study above, the problem was too much space, which allowed the pupils to be disruptive.

You also have to think about how you organize the pupils,

especially if the whole class is to be involved in the action. Pupils should not be allowed to wander around when they are not 'on stage'.

The lesson had got away from the teacher; it had lost direction, and he had lost control. The extent to which you, as the teacher, have to coordinate things will vary but, at least at the beginning, it is better to be prescriptive, even over-directive. As an NQT you simply can't afford to lose control of the situation and must keep a firm hand on the tiller. Later on, when a strong and successful relationship with the class has developed, you should be able to allow them to take more responsibility, but initially, you have to establish what good practice is.

It is undoubtedly more difficult to manage lessons where pupils move about than when they sit, more or less passively in their seats. Inspection teams have noted that some teachers are more reluctant to make use of this kind of lesson because it is harder to sustain good order. You need a good deal of confidence, because it means relinquishing some of your control over the pupils once they leave their seats. Our advice is to choose the time and the role play carefully and to prepare it well. If it is successful, it will considerably enhance the pupils' experience and help to motivate them. If you demonstrate that you can run an active lesson of this type well, the pupils will regard you as a really effective teacher and you will go up in their estimation. For a pupil's opinion of role play, read the final case study in the book, in Chapter 11, on page 203.

Managing Whole-class Discussion

A whole-class discussion can occur very frequently. Indeed most lessons probably incorporate a degree of whole-class discussion at some point since, clearly, it is a very good way of focusing everyone's attention on the topic, introducing a new idea, summing up events or the decisions of small group activity. It will be used regularly in such subjects as English, history or PSHE.

The most important aspect to remember about any class discussion is that it should be worthwhile for the whole class and for this reason it requires careful thought and planning.

Before embarking
Check that you have:

■   planned what is to be discussed

- thought about how you are going to organize the room
- thought about the order of events
- decided whether you require/ expect an outcome
- constructed a list of alternative strategies you could use if things don't go quite as you have planned!

Preparation

Establish some ground rules or procedures which are invariably applied. Do not be afraid to impose your own rules, which ought to include the requirement that only one person speaks at a time. Allow the class to contribute to formulating these rules during a preliminary session. You may require younger pupils to put up their hands if they wish to speak.

Decide whether the lesson will be entirely whole-class discussion or whether it might be more fruitful to allow small-group discussion first. This will, to a large extent, depend on the topic, and whether this lesson is part of a series, for example the introduction to a PSHE unit on drugs, or a 'one-off' to discuss charity events or the class entry for the school Drama Festival. This will also depend on the composition of the class – some groups are hopelessly lacking in self-discipline, while others seem to thrive on having the opportunity to talk to each other on a grand scale.

Think carefully about what your learning objectives are for the lesson. Try to clarify what you hope the class will gain from holding a discussion. Is it simply a question of exchanging views or information or are there some real decisions that need to be taken? Think too about how open the discussion is to be and what kind of lead you will give on potentially controversial subjects such as alcohol or contraceptives.

A row of desks may not be the most appropriate format for a successful discussion as pupils will be gazing at the back of other pupils' heads. A horseshoe or semi-circle tends to be the most effective seating arrangement to facilitate discussion, as pupils can see other pupils' reactions and expressions and the semi-circle helps to engender a feeling of intimacy and security. If it is a teaching space used by a number of teachers, you will need to check that you can rearrange the room, and you should build time for changing the room around into your plan for the lesson. You should also give some thought to where you will stand/sit. Are you going to remain doggedly at the front; should you retreat to a corner; and is it a good or a bad idea to sit down with the pupils?

Make a checklist of points that you hope will arise. Be

prepared, however, to think on your feet if the discussion takes a turn that you did not expect.

Managing the discussion

You want to engage the pupils' interest and attention right from the beginning. Consider using a case history to introduce the discussion, or a provocative statement written on the board, a newspaper article or possibly even a role play prepared ahead by a few of the pupils.

Once the discussion begins, you will want to ensure that it gets off to a good start. Allowing the more vociferous pupils to have their say will help you here, but try to encourage responses to their remarks. Invite others to join in by summing up what has been said and putting it into the form of a question, for example, 'So, do we agree with Sally that people who are HIV positive should be forced to declare it?' If you know the group well enough and are confident that you will not embarrass individuals, invite some of those whose hands do not shoot up to contribute. An example of a whole-class discussion based on questions is given in Chapter 6.

Do not be dismayed if some pupils do not speak. Certain topics, especially in PSHE, are controversial, sensitive and perhaps even beyond the experience, and therefore the scope, of some pupils, and makes it difficult for them to form or express an opinion. As long as everyone has listened, your discussion will have succeeded.

Try to discourage splinter group activity from developing, for example by saying, 'Philip and Ian – you seem to have strong views on this, why not share them with us. What do you think?' If the discussion becomes too acrimonious or personal, remind the group of the ground rules which encourage respect for others' opinions and, if necessary, reiterate that such opinions should never be personally vindictive, racist or in any way offensive. Keep a constant eye on the pupils, so that you can intervene or change the direction of the debate if you notice that a pupil is beginning to look upset.

Use your checklist to keep control of the discussion, using ideas to trigger discussion if a lull develops. It is essential however to be flexible, especially in a PSHE lesson, where the discussion may need to be wide-ranging. Always adapt and accept. Experience will help you gauge the use or value of digressions; initially you will have to experiment and see what happens. Sometimes the topic will be so broad that it will provoke many differing views; sometimes the group will have particular concerns, or individuals within the group will have special concerns which they want to discuss. Whole-group discussion is an inexact science; what is important is to develop the ability to respond to the group or to an individual in a way that shows that you are taking their ideas and opinions seriously.

Drawing the debate to an end in a way that makes the class understand what the discussion has achieved is another art you have to master. Sum up the main points (it is usually best not to mention individuals by name at this point). One method of dealing with sensitive issues is to offer the group the opportunity to revisit the debate at a later date or to discuss points with you individually after the lesson. At the end of the session always thank the group.

CASE STUDY 3.7. FOR ACTION

I find managing the class discussions in PSHE very difficult. Last week we were supposed to be discussing contraception as part of the sex education module. The Year 9 pupils were giggly and silly from the onset and I had difficulty in getting them settled, but I thought that once we got going, it would be all right, but it wasn't. There was always an undercurrent. Side discussions kept breaking out amidst laughter and then Ryan shouted out a really crude remark and this brought the house down. I found it difficult to control and I didn't really know what it achieved.

For action/discussion
What issues were raised by this case study?
What mistakes had this NQT made?
What advice would you give this new teacher and on what grounds?
Where could this NQT get help and support?

Many beginner teachers find managing whole-class discussion of sensitive issues very difficult. For a serious discussion of this nature you need to prepare the group in order to create the right climate. In this case study the ground rules for discussion had not been established. The class were restless and giggly and at no stage were they prepared to take the discussion seriously. In this climate the discussion never really had a chance, and our advice would be, don't attempt to hold a discussion if you can't settle the class. To expect things to get better as they went on was wishful thinking. Indeed an expectation appears to have developed that this was a lesson in which the pupils could muck about, be rowdy and that it was all a bit of a giggle, and this situation would need to be rectified before the teacher could attempt another discussion. Ryan, who shouted out the crude remark, was clearly testing this NQT to see what a pupil could get away with and how the teacher would react. He needed to be dealt with immediately, for example by removing and disciplining, so that the class could see that behaviour of this kind would not be tolerated.

Where rowdiness develops or the pupils are not prepared to listen to each other, you should try to analyse why this is happening. Is it how you are managing the start of the lesson, the organization/seating arrangements of the room, or other outside factors? In this case part of the problem stemmed from embarrassment about the subject matter. If the group can't cope with a whole-class discussion, you need to think about a different method of dealing with the subject matter, and your year head or the PSHE coordinator should be able to advise you here. A technique that can sometimes help is to get the class to write down their thoughts/concerns on a piece of paper and give them in. Of course some comments will be written deliberately to shock, but this method puts you in control as you choose which statements to use. You may also find that breaking the large group up into smaller groups for at least part of the time may ease the tension.

CASE STUDY 3.8. FOR ACTION/DISCUSSION

Another NQT had a rather different experience in delivering the same PSHE module:

> They just wouldn't respond, and I found I had to keep talking to cover the silence. It was like getting blood out of a stone.

A pupil in the group viewed things differently:

> It was so embarrassing. Mr Rogers often picks on me, and he did it again yesterday, He has this habit of saying, 'Well, Sonia, what do you think about. . . ?' If I wanted to tell him what I feel, I'd put my hand up. It's none of his business and all the others stared at me. I felt really embarrassed.'

For action/discussion:

What are the issues raised by this case study?

What are the main differences in the pupil's and the teacher's perceptions of the lesson?
What advice would you give this NQT and on what grounds?

Planning and Running a Practical Session

You can only run an effective and safe practical session, in which you achieve your learning objectives, if you have carefully planned the lesson beforehand. Practical work normally needs at least a week's forward planning, and many technical support staff will demand at least this much notice if equipment and chemicals, etc. need to be prepared for your lesson. If you dash into school at 8.30 on Monday morning expecting to order equipment for a practical lesson at 9.30, you are likely to be disappointed and will have to do some very rapid rethinking – a sure recipe for chaos!

Your starting point is to decide on the type of practical activity. This might involve:

- a teacher's demonstration
- individual practical work
- working in pairs or small groups
- use of computer simulations, etc.

Departmental schemes of work should give guidance on what type of activities to carry out with the various courses taught. Once you have decided, make sure, by checking with the departmental technician, that the equipment that you want is actually available. There is no use deciding to have 30 pupils carrying out individual investigations into the force needed to lift a sandbag, if there are only ten sandbags in the school!

Having decided on the type of practical activity, you must carry out a risk assessment. This is legally required under the Health and Safety at Work Act. Your department should have a policy on risk assessments. Important safety points may be written into the schemes of work, or you may have to consult the general risk assessments literature. If your HOD has not explained to you how s/he expects risk assessments to be carried out, then you must ask what the procedure is. If you are unfamiliar with an experiment you intend carrying out with a class, then try it out beforehand and ask for advice if necessary.

Having decided upon your activity and carried out a risk assessment, think about timing. You must leave time to give instructions and safety warnings and to tidy up at the end of the lesson. Do you want to summarize the class results before the end of the lesson? Do you want the class to write up the experiment during the lesson? What will you do with those pupils who finish early? Your colleagues will not thank you if you leave a laboratory or other practical room in chaos at the end of the lesson, because you mistimed how long it would take to complete the activities that you have planned.

CASE STUDY 3.9. FOR ACTION

Jenny's Year 7 class was carrying out an investigation into the changes that they could observe when different chemicals were heated. The lesson was going well, when one of the class told her that there was no more sodium chloride left at the side of the laboratory, where the different chemicals had been set out. There was no one in the prep. room area next door who could get it for her, but Jenny knew that there was another beaker of sodium chloride on the prep. room bench. She left the laboratory for some 30 seconds to fetch it. During this time, one of the class got some chemical in her eye when she took off her goggles. Jenny dealt with this very quickly and the pupil was not harmed, but her mother complained to the headteacher about Jenny's inadequate supervision of the science lesson.

For action/discussion:

What are the issues raised in this case study?
What would you have done in Jenny's place?
What advice would you give Jenny and on what grounds?
Where can Jenny seek support in this difficult situation?

CASE STUDY 3.10. FOR ACTION

Gurinder had decided to introduce the topic of heart structure to his Year 10 class by dissecting sheep hearts. To reduce costs he had asked the class to bring in the hearts themselves to the next science lesson. Only six pupils out of a class of 24 remembered to bring in the hearts, so Gurinder organized the class into groups of four. At this point three girls in the class said that they objected to dissections. Gurinder let them sit at the back of the class, but they quickly started to chat about a party that they were going to at the weekend. The other groups began work, but it quickly became clear to Gurinder that they were too busy arguing over who should actually carry out the dissection to bother following the instructions on the worksheet that he had given them. Some of the arguments were getting very noisy. In the end Gurinder made them stop the dissections and, to fill in the time until the end of the lesson, he got the class to draw a diagram of the heart from their textbooks.

For action/discussion:

How do you think the class viewed this lesson, particularly the pupils who had made the effort to bring in the hearts?
What mistakes had Gurinder made?
What advice would you give him and on what grounds?
Suggest an alternative way of structuring this lesson.

You may wish to compare this case study with case study 6.2, 'The Science Lesson' in Chapter 6.

Preparing Your Resources

CASE STUDY 3.11 FOR ACTION

I felt such a fool. I had this really good programme that I wanted to show the class, but it was right in the middle of the tape, and I didn't have time to wind it to the right place before the lesson. The video machine that I had to use didn't have a counter, so I had to locate the beginning of the programme by trial and error, and it took me ages to find it. The class got very impatient and rather noisy. It was difficult to keep them in order while I struggled with the video, and by the time that I was finally able to start the programme, they had lost interest and it took me a while to get them to concentrate. Then of course the bell went when we were only half way through the programme (NQT describing a recent lesson).

For action/discussion:

How will the pupils have perceived this lesson and why?
What steps should this NQT take to prevent it from happening again?
What does this case study indicate about the link between lesson management and class control?

It is the kind of disaster that has happened to us all at some time. You can't find the beginning of a programme, you can't get the machine to work, it has recorded at the wrong speed, someone has helpfully erased the programme you wanted to show, or worst of all, all the video machines are in use just at the time that you wanted to show the programme. Effective use of resources is a key factor in determining how well a lesson goes. Clearly, in the case study above, the smooth flow of the lesson was interrupted, and the momentum of the lesson and the goodwill of the pupils was lost. Using resources effectively largely depends on how well organized you are. You cannot just walk into a room and expect everything to be ready for you to use: you have to make sure through your own preparation for the lesson that all the resources are available and in good working order. So what do you need to think about?

■ preparing the room
■ using the black/white board
■ equipment, eg, videos, which have to be booked, testing equipment to check that it works properly
■ materials – handouts, worksheets, sets of topic books, visual aids, etc.

Preparing the Room

In primary teaching you will be a class teacher, which usually entitles you to a classroom or flexible space which is your teaching space and which you can arrange as you wish. In secondary teaching, if you are lucky, the department will have a room or suite of rooms dedicated for its use, and you won't have to be totally itinerant, but even if there are subject rooms, there is rarely one room per teacher, and you will not have sole use of a room but will have to share it with other teaching staff. This will affect the layout. If the room is yours alone, you can arrange it how you choose, but if it is shared, then the layout is a departmental decision. You can obviously alter it for an individual lesson, but would need to return the tables/desks to their original place again at the end of the lesson.

There is no blueprint for the ideal layout of a teaching space. Different groupings of the desks or tables facilitate different activities. For example, if you want to talk to the whole class for a lot of the time, you do not want the room arranged so that a lot of the pupils are sitting with their backs to you, because this will affect how they listen. If you are planning group work, lines of desks in straight rows facing the front are not the best design as this layout would make it difficult for pupils to interact, so you need to rearrange the room for different activities. What is important is that you think carefully about what design you need to make the lesson work. If, for example, the space is too cramped, acting will turn into chaos.

It is difficult even for experienced teachers to move desks and chairs without generating some noise, and you may worry about losing control at this stage, but a good lesson does not always have to be silent, and if you organize it carefully, you can manage noise and furniture or pupil movement so that it is not disturbing. It will help your relationship with your colleagues, however, if you remember to check beforehand that your lesson is not over or next door to a test, so that you do not disturb someone else's lesson.

You can reduce the problem by careful handling and clear instructions, eg, 'I shall want all the chairs to be in a semi-circle facing me. We shall move the desks to the side of the room out of the way. We shall do this one row at a time. Row 1 that's the right side, starting with John, lift your desks carefully and turn them to face the wall next to you ...' Complete the first part of this operation before you allow any more movement, and be firm about this so that the pupils get used to doing it properly. If you think that they are making too much noise, make this clear, for example by saying, 'I am sure that we can manage this operation more quietly than this. Let the next row show us how it should be done.' It is also part of teaching the pupils to handle all the school's resources with care and respect. Make sure that when you plan your lesson, you take account of the time that will be needed to rearrange the room at the beginning and the end, and allow five minutes or so for this, otherwise you may find that you have run out of time.

Using Your Black/White Board Effectively

When you were at college, your tutor will have emphasized how important it was to set the board out clearly, preparing it ahead of the lesson if possible. However, using the blackboard effectively is difficult precisely because you often cannot get access to the board before the lesson, either because you are teaching elsewhere or because the room is not available so, unless you are a demon artist, you will not be able to draw complex maps or diagrams on the board. Similarly it will need to be wiped clean at the end of the lesson, and if you write, 'Please leave', on the only board so that you can use a diagram again the following day, you will probably not only be unlucky but also unpopular. So, most of the time you cannot prepare a blackboard ahead. Indeed it might be better in this situation to do a large chart, which you can display by fastening it to the board, use an OHP, or provide individual handouts.

Your board is useful for setting out headings, short tasks or page references, spelling words which pupils find difficult, working out examples, drawing a simple sketch, or listing ideas or points, for example from a brain-storming session. Often you will have to do this while you talk, and it is not easy. You must try to be legible, writing large enough for pupils at the back to read, and reasonably straight.

Some ways in which to cope with the problem:

■ Use the pupils – you may find it helpful, especially if the discussion is complicated, to ask a pupil to act as board scribe and write the ideas onto the board. This is usually popular, but you will have to watch that a different pupil gets a turn each time.

■ Discuss with the pupils the best way to set out the board, eg, 'Shall we use a spider diagram or should we make a list?' or, 'Would this information be clearer if we set it out in columns?'

■ Warn the class if you are likely to fill the board more than once in the lesson and will have to keep clearing it. You may have to wait a few minutes while the pupils get the key points down on paper.

Organizing your Equipment

CASE STUDY 3.12. FOR ACTION

When I was on teaching practice I had to teach this topic. It was quite complicated, so I prepared a lot of OHP transparencies. They worked very well and I enjoyed teaching the topic. When I started teaching here, I was pleased to see it on the Year 9 syllabus as I had all these transparencies ready to use, but I could never find an OHP available and in working order. I could not use any of my transparencies, the children found the topic very difficult to understand and I found teaching it very hard.

For action/discussion:

What advice would you give this NQT and on what grounds?

This NQT had come face-to-face with some of the problems that a new teacher might have to surmount when s/he wanted to use some of the materials or approaches s/he had developed on teaching practice. If you want to use equipment effectively, the main things that you have to think about are as follows:

How do you ensure that the equipment is available?

You need answers to several more questions in order to make sure that the equipment will be available when you want to use it. For example, is there an OHP or video machine in the teaching room? Where is the nearest one? Are you allowed to move it? Who provides the videos or the OHP transparencies – is it your department or is there a central store? Do you have to book all of the equipment or just some of it, and how do you go about this? How does the booking system work?

Do you know how to work the equipment?

A lot of modern classroom equipment is complicated to operate and teachers who find themselves doing battle with machinery that they cannot manage tend to look very silly. Playing the class a video which sounds like gobbledy-gook because you have recorded it at the wrong speed, will not help your image, nor will trying to use an OHP which won't focus because you are pressing the wrong knob, or have the transparency upside down and back to front. If you want to use equipment, make sure that someone has shown you how it works, and this means booking a session with a competent member of staff or the appropriate technician. The case study at the end of this section will highlight how not to go about it.

Have you tested it and checked that it is working?

There is nothing more infuriating than trying to use a video machine and not being able to get the sound or the picture to work, especially if, had you checked, you could have booked a different machine or changed what you would do in the lesson. So, it makes sense to try out the equipment before the lesson. Sometimes this is simply not possible, but if you do manage to test the equipment, it will enable you to approach the lesson with more confidence and certainty that things will go well.

Will your demonstration work?

In practical subjects a demonstration may form a crucial feature of the lesson. Even if you are highly qualified in the subject, handling a demonstration will need class management skills as well as expertise in your subject. Case study 4.5 in Chapter 4 illustrates what could happen as you try to manage the experiment and the class at the same time. Demonstrations which do not work will have an adverse effect upon the pupils' perception of your competence as a teacher, whereas a carefully prepared and well-run demonstration is a good way of stimulating both interest and learning. An example of managing a very successful science demonstration may be found in case study 6.4 in Chapter 6. Demonstrations need careful rehearsal, indeed a dry run would help you manage things better and add to your confidence.

Is your material ready to show?

Case study 3.11 showed how not being able to find the place on the video wrecked an NQT's lesson. In the middle of a lesson, when you are having to manage a lot of different things at the same time, you will not be able to put things in order. You have to come to the lesson with your teaching aids arranged ready for use, and in the order that you want them.

Some things you should try to avoid:

■   Wasting the pupils' time, eg, while you set up an experiment which should have been ready.
■   Decreasing motivation – because you have lost momentum and they are bored.
■   Failure to meet expectations – they never got to see the programme.
■   Loss of respect – they regard you as a technical moron!
■   Loss of status – you always fail to book the video or the room. Mrs X always beats you to it and secures it for her class.

CASE STUDY 3.13. FOR ACTION

I couldn't work the machine but one of the pupils, Philip, was remarkably good at it, so I got into the habit of letting him take charge of the equipment. Then one day he was away and I was really stuck. The programme was essential to my lesson, but whatever I did, I could not get it going. The class was getting noisier and more fed up by the minute. Then Roger said, 'Let me try, Sir, I am sure I can make it work.' I was desperate by that stage, so I let him try, but he couldn't make it work either. He must have forced a knob too energetically and now they say that the machine is broken and out of use, and when my head of department found out that I had been letting the pupils work it, he was really angry with me.'

For action/discussion:

This case study is an object lesson in how not to do it. What advice would you give this NQT and what lesson management skills did s/he need to acquire?

Preparing Teaching Materials

The kind of teaching materials you may have to use in a lesson could include:

- worksheets/task cards — with the exercise or activities for the pupils to do
- briefing sheets — to provide the background information for an activity or role play
- supplementary information — to expand the basic information provided in the textbook
- source/stimulus material — to provoke discussion or add a dimension to understanding.

Preparing teaching materials can be demanding and time-consuming as you do not have the previous experience on which to base short-cuts, so you want to use your time effectively and try not to do too much. Remember that too much paper can be an instant turn-off, and that a scruffy, badly presented worksheet is likely to contribute to your class management problems rather than making things easier for you. It is not how much time it took you, but the quality of the product that will count with the pupils. However long it took you to produce a poorly presented, boring handout, it is likely to be left abandoned unread and unwanted on the desks at the end of the lesson, and even more likely to be turned into paper darts during the lesson. Remember too that if the handout needs to be duplicated by a member of the clerical staff or a technician, you must give sufficient notice, usually a few days. Too often pressure of other work turns us into last-minuters who need, yet again, to beg a favour from the reprographics technician. Too many such requests will get you a reputation for being a disorganized teacher who is never on top of the job.

Some questions to ask yourself at the planning stage:

■   Is using this type of teaching material the best way to achieve my learning objective?
■   What do I want to achieve from this item?
■   How do I present the material?
■   How can I use it in the lesson to its best advantage?
■   Can it be re-used? Will I need to collect it in, and does this affect what material I use (paper, card, etc.)?
■   Am I reinventing the wheel? Have I looked in the department filing cabinet or asked a colleague whether something of the sort already exists? Always check how your colleagues are teaching the topic – you are a member of the department team and should not be working in isolation.

Some hints for preparing a handout:

■   make it clear
■   do not allow it to become too wordy or crowded
■   match it to the pupils' ability level
■   check that the language is user-friendly.

The biggest compliment that a pupil can pay you is to ask to keep, or even better, to purchase the item.

Working out the Assessment Method

Even before the advent of the National Curriculum, from time to time you had to assess your pupils to check how much they had learnt and where they stood in relation to other pupils. Whereas in the past this was often done through an end-of-term or end-of-module test, nowadays assessment activities which involve observing or monitoring normal classroom activities will regularly be used. This means that when you plan your series of lessons on a topic, you will need to include assessment activities as part of the programme and that some activities will have to be used as assessment tasks. This all sounds rather daunting, so how do you go about it?

The main thing to take into account is that this is not an area where you should be working in isolation. Fitting assessments into the cycle of lessons and checking that they do actually test the skill or competence at the required National Curriculum level is a team operation done by the department at specific planning sessions. You may be asked to contribute, but you should not have to do everything for yourself. The department will have examples of schemes that they are currently using or used last year, so even where you are asked to work on a unit, you should have access to some models on which you can base your own efforts. Where you do have a choice, for the first few times it would be a sensible move to ask your HOD what s/he recommends. Assessment is discussed more fully in Chapter 7.

CHAPTER 4

Lesson Organization and Management

How you organize your lessons is the key to effective teaching. A lesson has two objectives:

- a successful learning outcome – the pupils will learn something
- pupil involvement in the learning experience throughout the lesson.

What do you need to do in order to achieve your objectives? What are the things that you need to manage well and which, taken together, will contribute to an effective lesson or series of lessons? Figure 4.1 illustrates the contributory factors.

It has been claimed that observing a good lesson is not the most helpful way of learning about lesson organization because the good teacher manages so well that it all looks easy and it is difficult to identify how everything links together and what things really take a great deal of time and effort. In this chapter the case studies, featuring the problems experienced by Robert, an NQT in the modern languages department at Bestwick Park High School, will highlight where difficulties may arise and suggest strategies which could solve his problems and improve his lesson organization. The questions for discussion have been put before the interpretation of the case studies or any advice, so that they can be used flexibly, ie with or without recourse to the analysis.

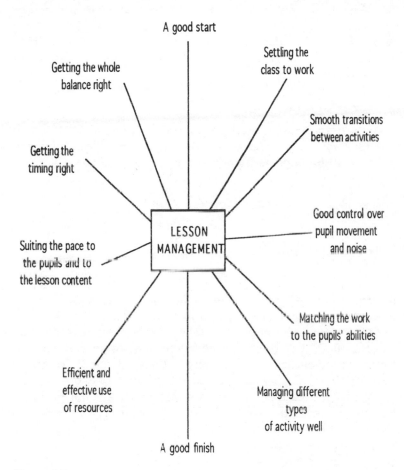

Figure 4.1

Starting a Lesson Well

How the lesson starts can be crucial in ensuring that you are in control and that pupils behave well and attend. The list below indicates some of the factors which will affect starting the lesson:

- Do you go to the class or do they come to you?
- Can you be in the classroom when they arrive?
- Do you have to collect books/equipment from the staffroom?
- Do the pupils arrive as a group or do they trickle in a few at a time?

- What lesson did they just have – does it affect their mood or time of arrival?
- What time of day is it? Are most of your lessons with a particular group late in the day and does it affect their settling down?
- How frequently do you teach the class and how recent was the previous lesson?

A successful lesson will start very shortly after the time stated on the timetable. Two factors contribute to this: your punctual arrival and the pupils arriving on time.

Your Punctual Arrival

Why should we arrive on time? Mr. Cave is never there when we arrive ...

If you want to ensure that the pupils are punctual, you have to set an example yourself. This is not always easy to do. For example, your previous lesson may be situated in a distant part of the school, you may need to change over books and equipment, and the pupils may be remaining in the same room they were in for their previous lesson. All or any of these factors could lead to you arriving late, hot and bothered. If only one of a class's lessons is affected this way, it shouldn't prove a major problem, but you will need to explain clearly so that the class understands that it will take you a few minutes to get to them, and you should try to develop some strategies to get the group started on some work while they wait for you. You will have to build this procedure into the weekly scheme of work. If you adopt this approach, make sure that from time to time you check what the pupils have done, or they will quickly stop bothering to do anything at all. Resist the temptation to stop on the way to the staffroom for a chat with a colleague, or to linger in the staffroom at the end of break, lunchtime or a free period, because if you do, you will quickly get a reputation for being late, and you will find that it will affect the pupils' attitude to you as a teacher as well as their own punctuality.

The Pupils Arrive on Time

CASE STUDY 4.1. FOR ACTION

Sorry we're late, Sir ...

Robert Cave taught his Year 9 class three times a week, in two double lessons and one single. The class always took a long time to arrive. The single lesson, which was the last period in the afternoon, was particularly bad. The pupils trickled in two or three at a time, saying, 'Sorry we're late, Sir, but we've had games and they always send us late to change ' As the term went on, it seemed to get worse. The lesson was being eroded by eight to ten minutes, and because the pupils arrived a few at a time, it was very difficult for Robert to start the session effectively. When he finally dared to complain to the games department, the PE teacher looked puzzled and commented that to the best of his knowledge, he had only run late once this term and that occasion had been very near to the beginning of term. 'They're trying it on' he said. 'You will have to put a stop to it!'

For action/discussion:

What are the issues involved in this case study?
How could you as an NQT deal with a situation in which the pupils arrive a few at a time and make it difficult to start your lesson?
What advice would you give Robert in this situation?
Where could he look for help or advice?

Unpunctuality on the part of pupils can arise for a number of reasons. These include:

- logistical problems – the pupils have to come from a practical lesson, eg technology, where clearing up may be necessary, or from a different building, or from different sets
- lack of enthusiasm for the lesson – lateness can be an indicator of the unpopularity of a topic or subject
- lack of respect for the teacher – pupil lateness is often an indicator that the relationship between the pupils and the teacher is not developing well
- the pupils are testing the teacher – they want to see what you will do, and whether they will get away with it
- your own poor punctuality – which encourages the pupils to be late and puts out signals about you as a teacher.

Poor punctuality can lead on to other problems in the classroom, so it should be dealt with and not allowed to continue, or, as Robert found, it will worsen and spread to include more and more pupils.

How do You Ensure Punctuality?

Establish what the expected standard is and keep to it
Make it quite clear from the start that you expect punctuality – lateness is to be the exception, not the norm.

Restate the rule so that no one can pretend not to know it
In Robert's case where the standard has slipped, he must restate to the class what time the pupils are expected to arrive, taking into account any allowance for lateness from games. You must be seen to be fair, but not a soft option.

Monitor the lateness
You should monitor: who, how often, how many minutes etc. and keep a clear record so that you do not become involved in an undignified and unproductive public argument with a pupil or group of pupils.

Apply sanctions
What should you do about the lateness? Time has been missed, so has work. Are both to be made up, or just the work? Should this entail your putting individuals or possibly a whole class into detention? Our advice is to be very wary indeed of a whole-class detention, especially in your first term or so of teaching. It could test your authority as a teacher, and your class control, to the limit, and end with a confrontation between you and a group of hostile pupils. Our advice would be to discuss the situation with someone more experienced, eg your mentor, your HOD or the year head, and work out what possible approaches you could take in dealing with the problem, so that the potential pitfalls can be avoided and any sanctions can be applied effectively. Remember never to threaten what you cannot be sure you can carry out successfully. However you go about it, it is essential that some action is taken, and seen to be taken, and it is important that the pupils are not allowed to get away with this kind of misbehaviour.

When the pupils see that you are not going to be messed about, they are likely to treat you with greater respect and improve their punctuality. Then any hard-line cases can be dealt with on an individual basis.

Always praise improvement

Show that you have noticed any improvement and praise the pupils concerned.

Settling Down to Work

A formal start to the lesson in which you greet the pupils and explain what is to be done in the lesson is probably the most effective way to begin. It will appear to the pupils as the most businesslike approach. It is important to establish a positive climate for learning and of course the first key task is to capture the pupils' attention. The list below aims to provide you with some hints on how to gain and hold the pupils' attention. The suggestions given here also apply to any section of a lesson in which you will wish to talk for any length of time to a whole class.

Hints for holding the class's attention

■ Stand in a prominent/central position where everyone can see you clearly.
■ Be prepared to wait for attention – but not too long.
■ Do not talk over noise – get the noise stopped when you wish to speak to the class, and establish this as a routine.
■ Be very clear – speak clearly and calmly. Vary the tone and pace, and perhaps, if you have a lot of instructions, vary the volume level as well. Try not to speak for too long – match the amount of time that you talk to the ability and concentration level of the group. Keep any introduction to a lesson short and simple.
■ Be purposeful – so that the pupils feel that the programme for the lesson or the task is an important and interesting activity.
■ Engage in eye contact with individual pupils.
■ Make sure that you look and talk to all parts of the room, not just the same point all the time. Scanning helps you secure attention.

■ Try to avoid unnecessary interruptions during this phase of the lesson, and if an individual needs attention, try to deal with him/her once you have settled the class to work. Similarly, if someone doesn't understand, establish the procedure that you will explain individually at the end of this section of the lesson.

So what do you do if the pupils genuinely can't all arrive at the same time and straggle into the room in groups over about ten minutes, for example from various technology/sports activities? There are a number of options open to you, including:

■ you could provide some short task that pupils can do while they wait, eg, answer three questions on ...
■ you could start with some reading/stimulus material that pupils can study while they wait
■ you could see pupils individually about work and get them to check through and correct work
■ you could establish a procedure in which the instructions are on the board or contained in a handout so that individuals can start work as soon as they arrive in the room, and make the teacher exposition a regular feature about ten minutes into the lesson.

Managing Transitions

Often during a lesson you will want to change from one activity to another. You may start with a short exposition to the class, then you may want the pupils to move their chairs into a semi-circle to watch a video, or form small groups for discussion or group work, or simply to open their textbooks and do some written work. Any change of activity can involve movement, noise, uncertainty and dead time and the opportunity for misbehaviour, for example when one child or a group has finished and has to wait for the next stage to begin.

How can you ensure the smooth transition between activities and avoid dead times? Here are some pointers:

■ Key up the stages of a lesson as you reach them, so that one section of a lesson links easily into another.
■ Don't rush things. Aim for smoothness, so that one activity leads on logically and clearly into another.
■ Have all your equipment working and ready to use – this prevents dead time, while the pupils wait.

- Advice about moving furniture with the minimum of noise is included in the section 'Preparing your room' in Chapter 3.
- If you have to issue topic books, information about the task or other materials, think about the most efficient way of doing this, so that you do not waste time or it is a long time before the activity can start.
- Do not be afraid of some noise. When you start a new activity, inevitably there will be noise – moving chairs, regrouping, changing over books, turning pages. Often there is a hum as pupils react to the new task. Don't depress a buzz of interest, but don't let it go on for too long. Allow a short time for the change-over, then signal clearly that the class or groups should be on-task, and that all noise should cease or that even legitimate working noise should be kept to a minimum.
- Issue instructions clearly and then get the activity going, ie don't waste time here. If a few pupils need further clarification, address them as a small group or as individuals, but let the others get started.
- Have extension work available for those who can be expected to finish early – this always helps avoid dead time. Remember to avoid it being more of the same.

Getting the Balance of the Lesson Right

CASE STUDY 4.2. FOR REFLECTION

Letter from Mrs Styles, mother of Amanda, 10F:

> Amanda has been taught German by Mr Cave this term. She likes his lessons, but we are concerned about the amount of time she has to spend working on this subject at home compared to her homework in other subjects, including her other foreign language, French. We have talked to Amanda about this and she tells us that they are having to do a lot at home because they don't get through very much work in class. Her friends say the same. We are not sure what is causing this problem, but feel strongly that something should be done ...

Memo from Mrs Gatlin, headteacher of Bestwick Park High School, to Marianne Polle, head of German, who is also Robert's mentor (copy to Roger Russell, head of modern languages):

I have received a letter from Mrs Styles, mother of Amanda in
10F, about the amount of time that Amanda is having to spend
working on German homework. Could you investigate, please?

It is important to get the balance right between classwork and
homework. It is Marianne Polle's responsibility in the first instance to
assess the situation, find out what the problem is and, together with
Robert, work out a solution. She must approach the situation
sensitively. Understandably teachers feel threatened when a parent
writes in complaining about an aspect of their teaching. It is Robert's
first term and the complaint is likely to worry him a lot and affect his
confidence. Marianne will obviously have to tell Robert that Mrs
Styles has written to the head and discuss the matter with him. One
approach she could take is to depersonalize the issue to some extent
by applying a problem-solving model in order to clarify the problem
and generate some solutions.

1. What is the problem?

The balance between class and homework has gone wrong in Year
10 – too much time has to be spent by the pupils working at home.

2. Analyse the possible causes

■ Disruption – pupils distracting others and preventing work from
being done.
■ Poor timing – not covering the work in the time allocated, eg, too
much content, or Robert is working much too slowly.
■ Wrong structure – introduction too long, working time too short.
■ Speed/pace not suited to the content.
■ Content not suited to the ability of the pupils, eg pupils find the
work difficult and progress slowly.
■ Loss of timetabled time for various external reasons so that the
syllabus is not covered.
■ Teacher loses sight of the objective and allows him/herself to
wander off the topic.

Marianne and Robert discussed the possible causes. She saw his
teaching file regularly and the work looked to Marianne to be
appropriately targeted, nor did she think that it was too much
content. The majority of the Year 10 pupils in the group had no
record of being disruptive and Robert seemed to like them. The
discussion provided an opportunity for Robert to say how he
perceived the situation, but his experience made it difficult for him to
pin down precisely what was going wrong. He thought the class was
a bit chatty sometimes and they seemed to work rather slowly.

3. Who can help Robert?

Obviously Marianne, who is both Robert's HOD and his mentor, is his best source of help, especially as his relationship with her is good. Discussing the problem with her helps Robert to be more detached and objective about it. Marianne, in turn, is ideally placed to check whether Robert's assessment of what is happening when he teaches the class is accurate. To do this she will have to observe some of his lessons with 10F. She saw three lessons over a two-week period. The observations indicated that although Robert's lesson structure was not always ideally suited to the topic being studied, this was not what was generating the problem, nor was it the pupils who were wasting time, it was Robert! The real problem was something that neither of them had considered – Robert was a distraction!

When Robert set the class a task, he didn't allow them to get on with it. He constantly interrupted them with comments, new instructions or more information. This affected class concentration. It often provoked responses from the pupils and pools of conversation broke out. This made it very difficult for the class to get on with the work and seriously affected concentration, so that, although a generous amount of time was being allocated in each lesson for the class to work on exercises, in fact very little of the work was completed. Then, at the end of the lesson, Robert would tag the unfinished work onto any homework he set so, not surprisingly, the class regularly had a lot of homework.

4. Generating a solution

Clearly once he had set a task or class activity, Robert had to make a determined effort not to interrupt the pupils or to disturb their concentration. Marianne also suggested that it might be quite helpful if Robert made it clear to the class how long each task should take, for example, 'This exercise should take you about ten minutes.' If he does not complete work in class, he must rethink homework, because it should not regularly exceed the time allocation.

5. Action

Robert now had to act on the suggestions and to try to discipline himself. Marianne had to report back to the headteacher and say what she had discovered and how the problem was being resolved. She would also monitor Robert's progress by returning to observe the class again in a fortnight's time to see whether things had improved.

What Does this Case Study Tell us about Lesson Management?

Several points emerge from Robert's experience with his Year 10 class:

- to manage a lesson well you have to be able to do a wide variety of things at the same time
- you have to watch yourself as well as your pupils
- too many interruptions affect progress.
- it is crucial to get the timing and the pace right
- you have to be able to monitor how well a lesson is going, react and adapt your lesson if necessary – good lesson management involves thinking on your feet
- it is important to get the overall balance of the lesson right.

Good Lesson Management is Like a Juggling Act

The list of possible causes of the problem affecting Robert's lesson indicated some of the variables that you have to take into account when managing a lesson. It was a long list and it is difficult, when you are a new teacher, to cope with all the things at the same time. It has been described, rather aptly, as a juggling act, where you have to throw the balls into the air and keep them all moving at the same time. It is certainly an art. Like the juggler's act, it takes a lot of effort and practice to get the lesson to look as if it is effortless and easy. At first it will be quite time-consuming, because you will have to work out all the things you have to take into account to ensure that the lesson works well, but as time goes on and you become more experienced, the lesson will become more of a cohesive whole and less the sum of its parts. Practice will bring improvement, and analysing and reflecting on your own practice, especially with your mentor, will help you.

Getting Your Timing Right

There is more to a good lesson than selecting content appropriately. It is about how you organize presenting the material and about breaking it down into 'bite-sized chunks' so that it can be digested by the pupils. Your syllabus is usually content-heavy, so you have to get through a lot of material in a short time. You will usually think that you have to cover it in much too short a time. Your department will probably have gone through each topic in the syllabus and allocated a set number of lessons or weeks to each unit. You will therefore have to work within that timetable, and cannot afford to run late, but you must not, as Robert did in the case study, fall into the trap of tacking the work not covered in the lesson on to homework. This means that timing is an essential feature of good lesson organization. You have to take the material you want to cover, or the various activities in a lesson, and work out what proportion of the lesson each should occupy.

It is often sensible to make it clear to the pupils how long an activity should take, because they are then partners in keeping to the timetable. Remember that if you do not tell them, they cannot be expected to know by instinct how long a task should take, and some pupils could think that they have the rest of the lesson to do an exercise that you expect to occupy only ten minutes. Another advantage of this approach is that you are helping the pupils to learn to work to time.

Don't Give the Impression that You are Running for a Bus

What should you do if you don't seem able to get the timing right? Do not simply nag the pupils, as this is likely to be counterproductive. Follow the example given in the case study above and try to analyse why this is happening, and work out how you can put things right. Perhaps you should think about the pace of the lesson. You do not want to give the impression that you are running for a bus, and likely to miss it. If you set too fast a pace and the lesson feels like a mad dash through a series of incoherent activities, very little learning will take place, and the pupils will become muddled, lose interest or get too tired to concentrate. On the other hand, you do not want the lesson to drag, so if the session seems to be moving too slowly, you should try to change the pace. Make sure, however, that it is appropriate to the learning needs of the class and to the demands of the materials.

How do You Deal with Interruptions?

CASE STUDY 4.3 FOR REFLECTION

Every time I reach a critical point in the story, Tina will say, 'I don't understand that, Sir, can you explain it?' I can't tell if she is really thick, or simply being difficult. Up to now I have answered her, but it ruins the whole effect, and I am beginning to find it very irritating. How should I handle it? (Robert is having a session on lesson management with his mentor.)

Interruptions can adversely affect both the timing and the pace of a lesson. They can also ruin the atmosphere that you have taken pains to build up, and can prevent progress. Some pupils have got it down to a fine art; others become confused and demand an instant explanation; so what do you do?

If you are really confusing the class, the signals will come from a lot of pupils and you would have to stop and clarify things, so this kind of interruption from one pupil indicates something about the pupil. In the case study above, Robert's starting point should be what he knows or can find out about Tina's ability and attitude. Do other staff have this problem with Tina and how do they handle it? Tina's requests for help or attention interrupt the flow of the lesson and, whatever the cause, Robert will have to establish that individuals will receive help at the end of this section of the lesson, and if Tina persists, he must check her. If the problem is genuine understanding, this approach should deal with it. Sometimes a pupil's lack of confidence leads him/her to seek attention. Robert should ensure that when he is free to spend time with Tina, he reassures her. He should also monitor how much of his time this one pupil is occupying. If Tina is taking up a great deal of time, Robert will need to consult the year head. If she is attention-seeking to prevent the class from making progress, this could also be a matter for consultation, so that the problem can be resolved.

Dealing with interruptions as they occur can often cause side-tracking and this can be very confusing for the pupils, who may lose sight of what are the main ideas being presented to them. So the advice to you as a new teacher is to establish a procedure which makes it clear that interruptions are not acceptable and that individual queries will be dealt with at the end of that section of the lesson.

The Exception Justifies the Rule

Don't worry if occasionally you forget to ignore the interruption and, before you notice it, you are involved in some kind of exchange that diverts the lesson from its intended path, and you think, 'Gosh, here I go again, that's ruined that lesson!' It does not mean that the whole lesson is ruined, or that the rest of your work with the group has not been worthwhile. Indeed the diversion may have been very valuable. What you have to ensure is that you don't let it happen too often, and that you do cover the syllabus. A good check is to make a brief note on your lesson record when a side-track occurs; this will monitor frequency for you and indicate if you need to take action.

Vigilance – Keeping an Overview

Some teachers are said to have 'eyes in the backs of their heads'. In reality they have developed a technique for keeping an overview of the class and picking up cues and signals which indicate to them what is going on. Jacob Kounin, an American researcher, has called this technique, 'withitness'. NQTs often miss these signals – they are so overwhelmed by all the different demands of the classroom, they miss the indicators which could result in an incident which could ruin the lesson.

How can you ensure that you are aware of what individuals are doing so that you can intervene before a disaster occurs? The technique which will probably help you most is 'scanning'. You should consciously scan the classroom, ie glance round the room every few minutes to monitor general behaviour and notice individuals. It is also a sensible move never totally to turn your back on the class for any length of time. For example, when you need to write on the black/white board, turn slightly sideways to the class.

CASE STUDY 4.4. FOR ACTION

Robert had been writing some questions on the board for the class to answer. Gradually he became aware of a soft noise towards the back of the class, but before he could turn round, a slightly misfired paper dart struck him in the back. 'Sorry, Sir,' said Darren. 'I meant it for Mary, but I got you by mistake.'
For action/discussion:

Robert had turned his back for too long – how could he have prevented this incident from occurring?
What advice would you give him in dealing with it?

CASE STUDY 4.5. FOR ACTION

'Can I open the window, Sir?' asked Suzi, 'It's very hot in here.' The teacher, preoccupied with trying to run a difficult experiment, nodded, but didn't watch her. Suzi pushed the window hard, right up to the top. A gale promptly blew in and Tony's worksheet blew out of the window. 'Shut it, you idiot! yelled Tony, clutching his possessions desperately as they scattered in all directions. 'Shut that window immediately!' shouted the teacher, noticing the incident, but reluctant to leave the experiment which was at a critical point. Suzi pulled on the window, but nothing happened, and it seemed to have jammed open. 'I can't move it , Sir,' she cried; wrestling with the window. Other pupils crowded round helpfully offering conflicting advice and the scene became increasingly chaotic. The teacher had to desert his experiment and try to close the window. Only then did he realize that Suzi had fastened the catch! When he released the catch, the window slid gently into place. The experiment was ruined.

For action/discussion:

How could this teacher have prevented the incident which ruined his lesson?
What advice would you give him in dealing with it?

These case studies demonstrated that good lesson management will help you with classroom control. The importance of lesson management skills has been highlighted by the research carried out by Jacob Kounin. He compared the videotaped behaviour of teachers who were regarded as having few discipline problems with the behaviour of teachers having frequent problems:

> What was particularly notable was that the former's relative success largely stemmed from their being simply more effective lesson managers, rather than from anything to do with how they dealt with pupil behaviour. (Kounin, 1970.)

The case study which follows picks up on this link between classroom control and good lesson management, but also indicates the extent to which you have to be 'with it' in terms of what is happening in the school.

CASE STUDY 4.6. FOR ACTION

Robert had an important topic to introduce to the class. Because he had been off sick with flu, he was behind schedule, but it was nearly the end of term and he was anxious to push ahead. So, on his first day back, he launched into the new piece of work, but his Year 10 pupils were chatty and inattentive. They seemed unable or unwilling to concentrate, made silly mistakes and seemed to regard the whole thing as a joke. Robert became increasingly irritated with the class. Jane and Sara were particularly silly, and when Robert asked Jane a fairly easy question, she made a complete hash of it and then burst into loud giggles. Robert, goaded too far, told her just how inadequate he thought her answer was, but this made her giggle even more loudly, and when he ordered her to stop the laughter, she, quite truculently, told him that it was his fault that she had got the answer wrong, because he never explained things properly. Robert said that it was not a matter of how he explained things, a 2-year-old could have answered that question better than Jane. Jane now began to mutter very loudly, under her breath, that it was rotten luck to have got a teacher who was always away and was no good at his job. Robert told Jane to leave the classroom immediately and to stand outside the door. He was anxious lest she defy him, but she finally went, loudly and taking her time about it. Her friend, Sara, called out, 'Shame, you're picking on her!', so Robert sent her out as well. Now the class was much quieter, but definitely hostile. Robert, doggedly getting back to work, found them sullen and reluctant to answer. Finally Philip spoke up, 'Sir,' he said, 'We don't think that you are being fair. Jane shouldn't have been rude, but you know that the school play is on all this week and she has got one of the main parts. It is no wonder she made some mistakes.'

For action/discussion:

What are the main issues in this case study regarding a) classroom management, b) classroom control and discipline?
Which do you think was the main issue here and why?
What does this case study tell you about the class's perception/assessment of their teacher and what problems does it indicate?
What advice would you give Robert?

Finishing Lessons

CASE STUDY 4.7. FOR ACTION

I have to teach in Room 8 after Robert has been there with his Year 9 class. It is cutting at least five minutes off my lesson every time, because his lesson always ends late. Then they come out rowdily, pushing my class, who have lined up outside the door, out of their way. When we finally get into the classroom, it is in total disorder and I have to spend the next five minutes or so picking up after 9B and putting the chairs and desks straight. By that time I am usually extremely irritable and so are 10C. I snap at them and the lesson gets off to a thoroughly bad start. I have mentioned it to Robert, and things got better for a while, but now it is just as bad as ever. Could you have a word with Robert, before I lose my temper with him? (A teacher has complained to Marianne Polle, Robert's HOD.)

For action/discussion:

What mistakes had Robert made?
What advice would you give Robert?
If you were in the position of the other teacher, how should you handle this kind of situation?
What are the lessons of this case study for an NQT?

Finishing a lesson successfully is as important as starting it well. It may seem surprising, but, unless you plan carefully, a lot can go wrong at or near the end of a lesson and this can ruin a lesson into which you have put considerable effort. Unfortunately it is the chaos at the end that will stay in the pupils' minds, not all the good work which went into the earlier part of the lesson.

The first crucial point is to allow enough time to do all that has to be done before the bell rings. Here are some things you have to do in the final stages of a lesson:

■ draw the topic to a close
■ reinforce what should have been learnt
■ set homework
■ clarify exactly what the pupils are expected to know or do before the next lesson
■ clear up and set the room to rights
■ dismiss the class in an orderly manner.

Bringing the topic to a close and summarizing what should have been learnt in the lesson is an important process because it reinforces learning and provides the pupils with a checklist of what they should take away from the lesson. Do not spend too long or labour it, as it will lose its effectiveness. This should lead you onto setting the homework, which usually arises from the lesson. Make sure that the pupils have grasped precisely what it is that they have to do: if the work has to be handed in or not, to what place it should be handed in and whose responsibility this should be, ie does each individual hand in his/her work separately, or is there a homework monitor who collects in all the books for your subject? If a pupil needs further explanation after the bell has gone, do this outside the room, so that the next class are able to enter. Sometimes it is useful to allow a class to start its homework in the last section of the lesson. It enables you to check progress and understanding of the task set, but this will vary according to what work you are doing.

Case study 4.7 highlighted several of the points that you need to get right in order to finish a lesson well. First there is the knock-on effect of running late. Robert's colleague was annoyed because he regularly lost time because Robert was always late finishing. It is actually better to finish a minute or two early than to overrun. The pupils will be wanting to leave from the moment that the bell goes, whether because you are eroding their free time by eating into their breaks or going on after the end of school, or you are making them late for their next lesson and another teacher will be displeased – again there is a knock-on effect. It indicates that you cannot get your act together, and the pupils will think of you as a poor organizer. Leaving the room in a mess for another colleague to clear up is a cardinal sin and one which will make you very unpopular. In a primary school you may be lucky enough to have your own classroom, but in a secondary school, even if there is a departmental suite, it has to be used by a number of teachers and they should not have to clear up your mess.

Another sin is to fail to dismiss the class in an orderly manner. It is basic good practice to control how the pupils leave the room. As a new teacher you may find it useful to have a formal procedure so that pupils know what to expect; for example - 'Please stand quietly and put your chairs under the tables.' At the end of the day you usually have to put all the chairs up on the desks to facilitate cleaning, so you must do this before you dismiss the class. Only when you are satisfied with the arrangement of the room, should you give permission for the class to leave. If you want to ensure that the pupils leave quietly, you can dismiss the class row by row or table by table once they have passed your inspection. This kind of ending to a lesson is far preferable to an unseemly and unruly scramble in which pupils elbow each other and any waiting classes out of their way in a dash for the door, toppling any furniture in their path. Controlling how the pupils depart will help you see that the room is left tidy. More importantly, it will help you not only to establish your authority, but contribute to building up your image as a competent teacher with high standards of conduct and work.

CHAPTER 5

Classroom Control

Establishing Your Authority

CASE STUDY 5.1. FOR REFLECTION

'If something isn't done about Nicola Philips, I'll strangle her in this afternoon's lesson.' Janice Lee, an NQT, has arrived in the deputy head's office in a state of extreme distress. The emotion she felt is one that many of you will have experienced at some time in your first years as a teacher. A pupil has managed to wind Janice up to the extent that she can't stand it any longer. She isn't seriously thinking of murdering Nicola, so what does she really mean?

First, she is expressing the extent of her exasperation with the pupil. She is also making it clear that the conflict between her and the pupil is reaching crisis stage. Her dramatic exclamation and her appearance in the deputy's office just before lunch are clearly a cry for help. She has got herself into a situation that she can't handle and she wants the deputy head to help her to get out of it.

This not uncommon scenario is all about Janice's authority as a teacher and her ability to handle pupils effectively.

For reflection:

What help does Janice need now in order to retrieve the situation? What should she do in future to avoid creating this kind of problem?

Retrieving the Situation

What is this problem about?

Some action will need to be taken urgently and certainly before the afternoon lesson. The first thing that Yvonne Perkins, the deputy head, is likely to do is to try to get the story straight. She will need to clarify why Janice feels so strongly, so that she can begin to understand what this problem is really about and assess the situation.

In this case the problem has been building up for some time. It started when Nicola, a Year 11 pupil, got behind with her homework. There is now a big backlog of assignments and Nicola, a bright, but unmotivated pupil, appears to have no intention of completing them. When Nicola failed to hand in her work, Janice set deadlines which Nicola didn't meet, and followed this with a series of threats, which Nicola, with increasing insolence, has defied. The situation has turned into a real battle of wills between the teacher and the pupil, and Janice is at her wits' end to know what to do next. She is afraid that when Nicola fails to produce any work in the lesson after lunch, she will have a crisis on her hands. Indeed there is a very good chance that Nicola will use the opportunity to make Janice look inadequate and foolish, and that if Janice fails to show that she is in control, it will undermine her authority with the other pupils in the group.

Who should deal with the problem?

Janice has appealed to the deputy head for help, but is she the most appropriate person to deal with this problem? Why has Janice gone straight to the deputy head? Surely Janice should have consulted her HOD, or the pupil's year head, dependent on the structure of the school. Has Janice targeted the deputy because:

- She doesn't know what procedure to use?
- She thinks that the HOD will be unsympathetic?
- She thinks that the HOD will have the wrong effect on the pupil?
- She doesn't want the HOD to know that she has a problem?
- She wants to be very tough on the pupil?
- She was desperate, and the deputy with her lightened teaching timetable was available when help was needed?

The answer probably lies in a combination of these factors. Janice would have said that she went straight to the deputy because of the urgency of the problem. In this case because it was so urgent and because Janice clearly feels that she needs strong support, the deputy head decided to initiate action herself, but made it clear to Janice that she would be informing the relevant section heads and involving them at a later stage, in monitoring the follow up.

What action should be taken?

The situation needs defusing and it must be made clear to Nicola and to others in the group that Nicola will not get away with her defiance of the teacher. However, this needs to be done in a way which will reinforce the teacher's authority, not undermine it.

In this case a message was sent to Nicola to report to Mrs Perkins' office at the beginning of the lunch hour. The deputy was particularly concerned to improve the working relationship between the teacher and the pupil as well as supporting Janice's discipline. She could fairly easily make Nicola do some work, but she did not want the pupil to become resentful and take it out on Janice. Thus when Nicola arrived, Mrs Perkins approached the situation from a discussion of the missing work, because if she highlighted Nicola's insolence, the pupil would immediately try ploys such as, 'She always picks on me', or 'Its not fair!' Instead, Mrs Perkins concentrated on getting an accurate picture of how many pieces of work were outstanding, and establishing that the work was going to be done. Nicola tried the usual gambit that she wasn't the only one with outstanding work: 'Other people hadn't done their work either ...', but it didn't help her because it was made clear that all the pupils in the set would be expected to complete the work, but Nicola had the greatest backlog and needed to extricate herself from that situation. The deputy pointed out to the pupil that anyone not doing work in her GCSE year damaged only herself and that the longer Nicola took about it, the more difficult she was making it for herself.

Mrs Perkins largely avoided recriminations about the past. Her interest was in when the work was going to be done. She was reasonable, realistic, but firm, which made it difficult for Nicola to argue the case or make a lot of excuses about why she hadn't done the work, and meant she did not have to threaten the pupil with further sanctions. Clearly three pieces of work could not be produced that afternoon, and Janice would have to retreat from that position, but one piece could be done by the next day and a realistic timetable could be established for the rest of the work. It was at this point that Mrs Perkins began to discuss Nicola's attitude with her, but although it was made quite clear that being sullen or defiant was unacceptable, this was largely done positively.

Once they had got that far, the deputy brought the teacher and pupil together to talk to each other and sort out the arrangements, making it clear that someone, probably the HOD, would monitor progress and see that Nicola kept to the timetable. Later Mrs Perkins had a word with the HOD not merely to put him in the picture, but to ensure that his sessions with Janice included looking at ways in which she could make her classroom control and authority over the older pupils more effective.

Had Janice got the support she needed?

Action had been taken at once to avert a potential crisis and to retrieve the situation.

Nicola would be going to the lesson that afternoon knowing that Janice had taken action to prevent any further defiance and that her authority was being reinforced by senior staff.

Other pupils knew that Nicola had been summoned by the deputy head and would rapidly realize that the situation had changed.

More importantly for the future, a working dialogue had been established between the teacher and the pupil. The deputy had established a framework and a more positive climate, but by getting the teacher and the pupil together, she largely enabled them to work things out for themselves.

What Can You Learn from this Case Study?

- Allowing a situation to develop can result in a crisis of authority.
- Pre-empt a crisis if possible.
- Sometimes it is useful to involve an intermediary, eg, the deputy head.
- The senior staff can't do everything for you, or your authority will collapse again once their presence is removed.

Discipline and class control is one of the major areas of concern for students and new teachers.

> The key to good discipline in the classroom lies in pupils accepting your authority to manage their behaviour and progress in learning. (Kryiacou, 1991.)

Particularly in the first few weeks of your teaching career, pupils will test you out. They will want to find out how good a teacher you are, what your standard is, what they can get away with and what you will do if they misbehave. It is essential that you establish your authority from day one in the eyes of the students, so how do you go about it?

You have to establish that you have adequate expertise in the subject

This does not mean that you have to know everything that there is to know about the subject, far from it. It would be most unwise to pretend to know about an area that you haven't studied at all — but you do need to be on top of your material and appear sure of yourself. You have to demonstrate that you are knowledgeable about your subject and interested in it. Your professional expertise is central to your authority and it is from your command of your subject that you derive your right to instruct pupils.

They have to respect your ability in your subject and if, particularly, the more able begin to suspect that you are at all unsure of yourself, for example that you are preparing one lesson ahead and only know what is in the textbook, they will give you a very rough ride.

You need to appear confident – to show that you have authority

Appearing confident, self-assured and firmly in control of the classroom situation will not be easy for you, especially in the first few weeks when you will be new to the school and somewhat unsure of yourself, yet those first few weeks are vitally important in creating a positive classroom climate. In a survey of teachers' first encounters with their classes, Wood and Wragg (for the DES Education Project) drew a comparison between the behaviour of student teachers and experienced teachers and, not surprisingly, noticed that the experienced teachers were much better at establishing their presence and authority, and generally were much more confident, warm and friendly.

It is important to be assertive, but be careful that your anxiety to make an impression does not make you aggressive: this could quickly lead to confrontations. Remember that acting with authority is not the same as being authoritarian and over-directive. Beware too of using a lot of humour in the first few sessions. Sharing a joke with a group is a mark of confidence, but it will take a while for the class to understand when you are joking, and you don't want them to laugh *at* you instead of *with* you. Basically you have to show that you are in charge and that you expect to be treated with respect.

Establish clear ground rules and enforce them

A well-ordered classroom will help you establish your authority and this involves setting up clear ground rules. It is important for the pupils to know what conventions and procedures to follow and what is expected of them. The majority of the pupils dislike uncertainty or confusion and respond positively to a clear code of behaviour. Below is a list of the rules or routines that Wood and Wragg identified via their classroom observations as the most commonly used. They are reproduced here to help you reflect on what routines you will need to establish in your own classroom. Remember that the pupils will respect those rules only if you consistently enforce them.

- No talking when the teacher is speaking.
- No disruptive noises or calling out.
- Procedures to be followed when pupils enter, leave or move about the classroom.
- No interference with the work of others.
- Specific rules for how work is organized and completed.
- Pupils must not shout out; for instance they must put up a hand when they want to answer a question.
- Pupils must make a positive effort in their work.
- Pupils must not challenge the authority of the teacher.
- Respect must be shown for property and equipment.
- Pupils must ask if they do not understand.

Teaching Competently is the Key to Classroom Control

If you can create a good working relationship with your teaching groups, you will avoid most of the discipline problems which you might otherwise encounter. A purposeful and task-oriented approach will get you off to a good start. A well-prepared and well-delivered lesson, not interrupted by unnecessary hold-ups, will help you establish the positive relationship with the pupils that is the key to effective classroom control. The atmosphere you aim to create should harness and support the pupils' willingness to learn and their interest by the presentation of the material, its suitability for the age and ability of the learners and the positive reinforcement that you provide through interaction with individual members of the group.

Even if you turn out to be a naturally talented and extremely effective teacher, you must expect to encounter some pupil problems.

Most pupils want to learn and will work for teachers who are interesting, interested in them, knowledgeable, consistent, fair and have a sense of humour.... It is also true that some pupils will pose problems whatever the circumstances and however outstanding the teacher. (Howe, 1993.)

Dealing with Discipline

What Kind of Pupil Problems Should You Expect?

■ Noise – difficulty in establishing/maintaining quiet in the classroom.
■ Lateness to lessons – prevents you from starting your lesson on time, or wrecks the start.
■ Work avoidance – poor concentration, not paying attention, reluctance to do the work, effort put into doing the minimum.
■ Disruption – activities designed to interrupt/disrupt the lesson, such as calling out, noisy or unruly behaviour, eg, with equipment, dropping things, slamming desk lids, etc., hindering other pupils to prevent them working or to prevent the class from getting on.

All of these are fairly minor 'crimes' in themselves, but become serious if they are not challenged and pupils are allowed to get away with their disruptive behaviour. If this happens, you are likely to find yourself trying to cope with several of the misdemeanours at the same time, and probably more serious behaviour as well. More serious misbehaviour includes:

■ Refusal to accept your authority – cheek, defiance, disobedience.
■ An incident between two or more pupils.

This kind of misbehaviour is rarer than the less serious incidents, but will become more likely if the more trivial misdemeanours have gone unchecked or allowed to become commonplace. Most serious incidents occur when a state of tension has built up between the teacher and one or more of the pupils as illustrated in the case study at the beginning of this chapter.

What Causes Pupils to Misbehave?

There are three major categories of causes of pupil misbehaviour.

1. **Causes Connected With How You Teach:**
   - Pupil boredom – your topic or approach fails to stimulate interest or your timing is imperfect and after a while the pupils lose interest.
   - Poor teacher organization/low pupil expectation of what you will provide – eg, your visual aids won't work or there are too many interruptions to the flow of the lesson so that the pupils get the message that you are incompetent, ill-organized or don't care.
   - Work incorrectly targeted – eg, too difficult, not challenging enough, needs more concentration than the pupils can manage, expressed in inappropriate language or it is unclear what the pupils have to do.
   - Insufficient support or positive stroking – giving feedback in a way that encourages the pupil supports a good classroom relationship. Tied into this is setting realistic goals for the pupils so that they achieve the targets and see progress. This will help motivate them and make them want to work.
2. **Historic Problems**
   - Poor attitudes and low expectations – inherited from a bad relationship or history of failure with the previous teacher.
3. **Causes Outside Your Control**
   - The pupil's personal problems – the emotional 'baggage' that the pupil brings with him/her. The pupil may have problems which make it difficult for him/her to concentrate or cope with the demands of school life and academic work. It may also be the only time that the pupil can relax. This means that work will not be the pupil's top priority and it could lead to attention-seeking or disruption of lessons.

How Do You Cope with Pupil Misbehaviour?

CASE STUDIES 5.2–5.4. FOR ACTION/DISCUSSION

Case study 5.2. 'Take your coats off!' – a problem in two parts

Part 1

It was the rule at Bestwick Park High School that pupils do not wear their coats in the classroom. It was a constant cause of friction because the pupils did not like leaving their coats on the hooks in the cloakroom as there was a tendency for property to go missing. This meant that they preferred to carry their coats around with them, and the easiest thing to do was to wear them. Where they knew that the teacher would notice and say, 'Take off your coats!', they usually took them off on arrival in the classroom, but where they thought the teacher wouldn't notice and didn't care, the class would keep its coats on.

For NQTs, dealing with coats can become another skirmish in the battle for control. 'It takes me several minutes to get them to remove their coats before we can start work,' complained Chris, an exasperated NQT. 'It is becoming a ploy to delay the start of the lesson. They see it as a game, and I don't know what to do, because the school rules state clearly that coats may not be worn in the classroom.'

For discussion:

What advice would you give Chris and on what grounds?
What are the issues raised by this case study?
Where can Chris get help/advice?
How would you deal with this kind of problem?

Part 2

The class arrived reasonably promptly. It was a bright spring day and very few were wearing coats, so getting the class into shape did not take long. Then Chris noticed that John was still wearing a non-uniform jacket so, having started the class on an exercise, he went up to John and said, 'Please take your jacket off, John.' John started in his seat. He had been miles away – there had been a big row the night before with his mates, Mike and Steven, and John was worried in case they would be waiting for him at the end of school and unsure what mood they were likely to be in. He reacted to the teacher's intrusion on his thoughts. 'No,' he exclaimed, 'I won't take it off.'

Chris was nonplussed. John was a very low-ability pupil, but normally he was extremely quiet and did not give trouble. John's defiance of the teacher had been so loud that the whole class, which had been working quietly, had heard it. They now stopped work to listen to what was clearly going to be a major confrontation between the teacher and a pupil. Chris realized that everyone was watching to see how he fared. He thought that the best thing to do was not to let the class see how worried he was and to keep things as low-key as possible. He tried again, patiently and without raising his voice. 'Come on John,' he said, 'You know what the rules say – no coats may be worn in the classroom. Take your jacket off now, so that we can all get on with our work! Just put it on the empty chair next to you.' Without meaning to, Chris made a gesture towards the desk and John must have thought that the teacher meant to remove the coat forcibly and he hit out at Chris. The blow caught Chris on the chest, winding him slightly.

The class was utterly silent now. They knew that John had gone too far, and were clearly wondering whether the teacher would know what to do. Pupil and teacher looked at each other for a moment or two, neither spoke, then Chris turned away from John and addressed another pupil: 'Anna, you are form captain, please will you go and find one of the deputy heads and ask them to come here.' 'Yes, Sir,' said Anna and went out. Chris turned his attention to the rest of the class. 'Just get on with your work,' he said quietly, 'I want that exercise finished by the end of the lesson.' Chris noticed that one or two pupils nodded, as if agreeing with the strategy he was adopting. He wasn't sure whether to say anything to John or not. The boy was just standing there irresolutely. Chris suspected that John was as surprised as he was at what had occurred and that he didn't know what to do. Chris would have liked to have spoken to John, but he wasn't sure that the boy could cope or what his reaction would be, so he said nothing and just waited for the deputy to arrive. Luckily one came quickly. The deputy, who had been briefed about the incident by the form captain, didn't ask questions in the classroom, he simply requested John to accompany him to his office. Everybody watched to see what John would do, but the fight seemed to have gone out of the boy; he just shrugged and followed the deputy out of the room. 'Come and see me as soon as you are free,' the deputy instructed Chris as he left. 'We'll sort it out then.'

For action/discussion

In what category of pupil misbehaviour does this case study fit?
What are the issues raised by this case study?
What were the strategies open to Chris?
How well did he deal with this situation?
What would you have done and why?
How should this situation be resolved?

Case study 5.3

Ian was already well into his exposition to the class when Gary finally arrived, late as usual. He came in noisily, greeting his teacher with the words, 'Sorry sir, I was held up by another teacher.' Ian sighed; investigating this excuse could lose the class a lot of time, not doing so could appear a sign of weakness. He compromised: 'We'll discuss it at the end of the lesson. Sit down, Gary!' Gary started towards the back of the room, then appeared to change his mind and sat right in the middle of the empty front row, constituting a physical barrier between the teacher and the rest of the class. As usual he had none of the right equipment, so a few minutes later he got up from his place and, interrupting Ian's exposition yet again, he walked over to Sharon's desk. 'Lend us a pen, Sharon,' he said, taking the one she was using out of her hand. Sharon began to protest and Ian had to intervene to restore order. By now the smooth progression of the lesson was disrupted and Ian found it difficult to keep the class concentrating, so as soon as he could, he set them to work.

As usual, Gary tried to use this as an opportunity to distract others, but finally he appeared to have started to work, then, just as Ian was helping Jeremy with something he found difficult, he thought he heard Gary make a very rude comment to the pupil behind him. Ian couldn't be quite sure what Gary had said, but he suspected that Gary had meant him to hear....

For discussion:
All teachers have to deal with some disaffected pupils.

What are the issues raised by this case study?
What strategies are open to Ian?
Who can help him?
What advice would you give him and on what grounds?

Case study 5.4

Whenever we start a new topic that I have prepared carefully and would expect to appeal to them, there is a group in the class who always say, 'We've done it already Miss, with the last teacher.' I can't find anything in Mrs Artimati's file that tells me anything of the sort, but I can't convince them and I don't know how to deal with it. Every few minutes one or other of them exclaims, 'Do we have to do this, Miss? It's boring. We've done it before.' It spoils every topic for me and for the rest of the form. (Dispirited NQT talking in the staffroom.)

For discussion:

In what category of pupil misbehaviour does this case study fit?
What are the issues involved in this case study?
How could a mentor help this new teacher?
What advice would you give this NQT to help him/her deal with this problem and on what grounds?

Some Hints for Staying in Control

Effective discipline rests on competent teaching and on the skilful use of strategies to avoid or deal with indiscipline. You will need two kinds of strategies – one for pre-empting misbehaviour, and one for dealing with it when it occurs.

Notice and have strategies for the things that, however illogically, are known to affect pupil behaviour, eg, your lesson is timetabled for the last period in the afternoon when concentration is at its lowest. Sometimes you will have to react to situations that have occurred during the day – for instance an incident in a previous lesson, or the weather has prevented the children from going outside at break or lunchtime, or when there has been a fire alarm or bomb scare and the pupils have become overexcited and restless. Be aware and be prepared to adapt your lesson. Similarly, if you become aware that attention is slipping, vary the activities and/or the pace of the lesson to preempt a behaviour problem from building up.

Be consistent – this relates to the advice given earlier in the chapter on having a clear set of ground rules and working to them. Children recognize and exploit inconsistency. If you have to deviate from your own rule, make it clear to the class why you are making an exception.

Monitor what is going on in your classroom. Scan the room from time to time so that you can see if any problems are occurring. Making eye contact with individual pupils will indicate to them that you are aware of what they are doing, and your body language will indicate what you think about a particular pupil's actions. Signalling in this way can help to nip misbehaviour in the bud.

Circulate from time to time so that you can check up on what is going on and you don't become too remote from the activity in the classroom. If you are in the middle of talking to the class and you notice a pupil or pupils not attending or talking, do not interrupt what you are saying, but go and stand next to those pupils, so that they know that you are aware of them. Touching a pupil on the shoulder for example, is a very risky strategy, and secondary teachers should never resort to it.

Whenever you notice misbehaviour, do something about it, otherwise you are signalling to the pupils that you are prepared to accept disrespect or poor behaviour. You may not wish to interrupt the flow of a lesson for this, so choose when you want to deal with the matter.

Don't let a problem build up, either by trying to pretend it doesn't really exist, or by not tackling it. The longer you leave a behaviour problem, the worse it is likely to get, until you reach a state of tension that could result in a major incident.

Beware of stirring up pupils. Stay calm and quiet. Try to avoid over-exciting the pupils or being loud yourself. Noisy teachers often make pupils noisier, and once they get into this state, it is difficult to retrieve the situation.

Don't fall into the trap of nagging the pupils; it tends to turn off even those who are basically on your side. You will have to reprimand pupils from time to time, but it works better if you simply emphasize what is required, reinforcing it with eye contact or by standing near the pupils concerned, and then getting on with your lesson.

Criticize the behaviour, not the pupil. Try to avoid the pitfall of personalizing things because, if you do, it is more likely to result in a confrontation or an ongoing clash of personalities, because the pupil will nurse a grievance.

Try not to let the pupils see that they have riled you. Stay calm, because if the pupils see that you are irritated or that they have upset you, they will realize that you are losing control. If they succeed in making you lose your temper, they have won. Resorting to sarcasm only tends to make a bad situation worse. Talking to someone else about the problem often reduces it to size.

CASE STUDY 5.5. FOR REFLECTION

A problem shared is a problem halved?

> Whatever they told me at college, it can be very difficult to tell another member of staff about a problem with a pupil (NQT).

Confiding your difficulties to another member of staff can be helpful for all kinds of reasons, including:

- a shared problem becomes more manageable
- it gets it out of your system
- discussing it helps you to clarify the issues
- your colleague may have had similar experiences to share and suggestions to offer
- the pupil may be causing difficulty in other classes besides yours.

Yet it can be very difficult to share a problem of this type because:

- people are busy and you don't want always to be asking for help
- pupil misbehaviour affects your self-esteem
- you need confidence to admit to problems, especially in your first term
- you don't want to be labelled as unable to cope
- bringing in a senior member of staff can be perceived by pupils as a sign of your weakness
- short-term contracts put pressure on teachers with the result that they become reluctant to admit to problems and anxious to keep up pretences.

However difficult, the advice remains the same – don't try to deal with a difficult or complex problem entirely alone. If the idea of consulting your HOD or a member of the senior staff worries you, the pupils' form tutor is often a good person to talk to in the first instance.

CASE STUDY 5.6. FOR ACTION

> It had become a real battle of wills. There were six of them. They sat in the middle facing me and they totally dominated things. If I asked Anita, David or Paul a question, Cheryl or one of her friends would answer. They were large Year 10 girls, raucous and generally uncooperative, real know-it-alls. They scored off me and the other pupils whenever possible – we all suffered. Yet I had to be very careful what I said to them, because they were quick to cry racism if things didn't seem to be going their way. I tried

reshaping the layout of the room, but this was difficult as my subject is science and the benches are fixed. I tried moving my position from the front, but they dominated the room wherever I stood. I simply don't know what to do. (NQT.)

For action/discussion:

What are the issues involved in this case study?
Why should the NQT definitely seek advice about this problem and from whom?
What advice would you give this NQT and on what grounds?

CASE STUDY 5.7. FOR ACTION

It is not exactly misbehaviour, but whenever Sonia and Tracy are inattentive and I have to reprimand them, they say, 'But you let Ellie do that, why can't we?' There had been a run of small breakages in the lab that they claim were 'Ellie's fault', and sometimes, when I am busy with some apparatus, there are little spurts of laughter or noise, and they say it is something that Ellie has said, but I don't see how she could always be the culprit, besides she is such a quiet girl. Then when it comes to group work, no one seems to want Ellie in their group, and it holds things up while I get it sorted out. They are in my tutor group and Ellie seems very reluctant to mix in or to do things. She's fairly new. The family are half-French and were living in France until recently. Ellie has a bit of an accent and I have heard the other pupils tease her about it, though it all seemed good humoured. Then Ellie's mother came to see me and said that Ellie was very unhappy and didn't want to come to school because Sonia and Tracy were bullying her. Apparently they pick on her all the time, take her things, make nasty comments to her and nastier ones behind her back and jeer at other pupils if they partner her in lessons or even have her in their group, so that others are afraid to have anything to do with her. I don't know what to think or what I should do about this situation. (NQT)

For action/discussion:

What is happening in this classroom?
What are the issues involved in this case study?
Why should this new teacher seek advice and from whom?
What advice would you give this NQT and on what grounds?

CASE STUDY 5.8. FOR REFLECTION

It started as the bell went. Charlene and Donna seemed to be arguing a bit as they began to collect their things together. I think it was about what a boy in Year 11 had said about one of them. They are always very loud and I didn't think it was anything serious. Anyway I thought that once they reached their next lesson, which was PE, their row would quickly be forgotten. Then suddenly I became aware that a fight had broken out. They were shouting abuse and really laying into each other, and the others, the girls in particular, were loudly egging them on. It had escalated in a matter of seconds. I tried to separate them, but they took no notice, and although they were only 14, they seemed much stronger than me. I couldn't make them stop. The hair was being pulled out in tufts. It was really unnerving, I didn't know what to do to stop it. (NQT describing the less than perfect end to a lesson.)

A major incident like this is difficult for any teacher to deal with, however experienced. As a general rule it may be helpful to realize that girls fight less frequently than boys, but their fights can be harder to stop and nastier. This incident didn't arise from poor quality teaching or the boredom factor, rather it arose from two girls needling each other at the end of a lesson as the pupils left. A few seconds later and it would have been on a corridor and someone else's responsibility. Although it might have been wiser to have told the girls to stop the argument and go to their next lesson, you couldn't have been expected to guess that it would escalate in the way that it did. When the fight started, you clearly had to deal with it, but what should you do to get an incident of this type stopped? The advice must be – send for help as fast as possible. Trying to break up this kind of battle on your own is too difficult, as it is likely to need at least two members of staff to get the girls apart. You may also need a witness because you cannot stop a serious fight without touching a pupil and this could involve you in a different kind of problem altogether. The combatants need to be separated and isolated as fast as possible and the crowd dispersed to its next lesson. So don't try to be a single-handed hero/heroine – you are more likely to get yourself thumped inadvertently because you are in the way. You should select the most reliable pupil/s and send for a deputy or to the staffroom for help.

CASE STUDY 5.8. FOR ACTION

'I won't do it! It's baby's work,' Darren shouted. 'You can't make me do it, Miss!' and pushing his books aside, he got up and ran out of the classroom. Angela is left facing the class. Whereas previously 8B have been working rather too noisily for perfect class control, but relatively good-humouredly, the children are now ominously silent, hushed, watching the teacher. Finally Lisa White spoke, 'What are you going to do now, Miss?', she asked. 'Aren't you going to try to get him back?'

Angela Jarvis is facing the most dramatic incident of her first term teaching at Bestwick Park High School. What should she do to cope with this situation?

What Should She Do about Darren?

Angela has here two immediate and interconnected problems. One concerns 8B, the other concerns the missing pupil, Darren Shaw. She hasn't yet settled down to a comfortable relationship with 8B, and, after half a term, she still feels that they are testing her out every lesson. Now they have a ringside seat at a clash between Angela and a pupil, in which the pupil has totally refused to do the work that Angela has set, shouted at the teacher and fled from the classroom. They seem to think that she should be doing something to get Darren back, but this course of action is fraught with difficulty for her. If she pursues Darren, Angela will have to leave 8B unattended. This could be most unwise because not only was she not supposed to leave a class in her care, her relationship with the class is not good enough for her to rely on them to behave sensibly while she is out of the room. Moreover finding Darren could take her a long time as he could be anywhere on the school site. As he lives on the estate bordering the school field, it is not impossible that he could have run off home. Even if Angela can locate Darren, can she persuade him to return and how would 8B view it if she has to come back without him? Failure to retrieve Darren would only add to her difficulties.

Where Should She Seek Help?

Although superficially tempting, searching personally for Darren is too dangerous to be attempted, so however badly it might reflect on her competence as a teacher, Angela will have to report him missing. Logically she should appeal either to her own HOD or to Darren's year head, but both were likely to be teaching, and she could lose another pupil searching for help. The person most likely to be free was one of the deputies. Little as Angela might relish revealing to a senior member of staff that she has lost a pupil, it seems the only viable course of action given that the problem was both urgent and serious. 8B are still waiting to see what Angela will do. She realizes that she must not let them provoke her and must not allow them to seize the initiative so, as calmly as possible, she answers Lisa's question. The information that she is sending for Mrs Perkins, the first deputy head, acts powerfully on 8B – they know that Mrs Perkins won't stand for any nonsense. Selecting Jenny Dixon, the most trustworthy member of the class, to fetch the deputy, Angela scribbles a hasty note. She also realizes that the best method of containing 8B is to keep them busy and to keep things as normal as possible. 'In the meantime,' she says firmly, 'get on with your work; we have lost quite enough time. It will mean a lot of homework for you, if you don't get most of the work done now.' Slowly and reluctantly the class begin work again.

Finding Darren

When Yvonne Perkins arrives, Angela explains that Darren has fled from the room and now could be anywhere. One or two of 8B raise their hands with helpful suggestions as to Darren's whereabouts, but Mrs Perkins laughs and says that she thinks she will manage to find Darren without undue difficulty. 8B believe her. Mrs Perkins has a well-deserved reputation for being firm, fair and extremely efficient. They accept that once she starts looking for Darren, he is unlikely to be missing for long. When a search of the lavatories and known hiding places in the school proves fruitless, Mrs Perkins rings home and when Darren answers, she instructs him to return to school immediately and report to her, otherwise she will have to contact one of his parents at work and ask them to go home and bring him in. Darren, understanding the implications of this, returns to school post-haste.

The Reckoning

The moment of reckoning has now come for both pupil and teacher. For Darren, having to report to the deputy means trouble – he has defied a teacher, fled from the classroom and gone out of school without permission. Angela, however, will have to explain how the incident arose and it will reflect on her competence in dealing with less-able pupils, her class control and her relationship with 8B. For an NQT on a short-term contract, this incident could spell disaster.

Darren is a very slow learner, but his explanation to Mrs Perkins makes it clear that he regards the worksheet that Angela has given him, when he could not cope with the work that the class was doing, as 'baby's work'. In his eyes it set him apart and made him look stupid. It is too obviously different from the work being done by the other pupils and the language and style seem to be pitched at younger pupils. He resents this intensely and also resents the fact that a woman has done this to him. He feels that she hasn't treated him with respect. 'She was right out of order, Miss,' he says to Mrs Perkins.

For action/discussion:

Into what category of problem does this case study fit?
Analyse the issues raised in this case study.
What are the lessons for an NQT?
Comment on how this incident was handled.
The incident will need to be resolved. Suggest possible solutions to the problem. What do you think would be the best possible outcome and why?
What advice would you give Angela?

CHAPTER **6**

Communicating in the Classroom

Key Elements of Communication

CASE STUDY 6.1. FOR REFLECTION

The Year 9 pupils arrived. As usual they had come in dribs and drabs and took a while to settle. The teacher, Miss Gibbs, tried to avoid any loss of time by setting the pupils a task which they could work on individually while the others arrived. It was a Key Stage 3 history lesson about railways and the teacher set five questions based on the chapter in the class textbook, so that the pupils would begin to read about the topic and assimilate and apply the information while they waited for the whole class to assemble. She had allowed ten minutes for this activity, and then she planned to take answers to the questions and use them to build up the story of how railways had developed in the nineteenth century. Towards the end of the time she had set aside for the written work, she went round the class to see what the pupils had made of the task. To her annoyance, yet again this mixed ability class had done what she hated most. The problem was not that no one had done the work – most of the class had completed at least two or three of the questions – but how they had done it. Most of the pupils had answered the questions by copying chunks out of the textbook. 'I've answered the questions, haven't I?' said Donna, when Miss Gibbs protested. 'Look, there's lots of writing – what's wrong with it?' demanded Freddy. Their resentment at being asked to think for themselves was very clear. What could the teacher do about this?

This case study highlights the main challenge for any teacher — it is to engage the pupils' attention and interest, and to make them willing to undertake the higher order tasks which involve thinking for themselves and using their initiative. In the case study the teacher had clearly failed to motivate the pupils — they did not rush to the lesson, rather they arrived in dribs and drabs — and they were slow to settle. They did not actively rebel, but their interest was not engaged. They did the exercise dutifully and mechanically. They had realized that they could get away with copying almost mindlessly and that this would pose a much greater challenge to the teacher's authority than refusing to do the work. What could Miss Gibbs do about this situation?

Communicating in the classroom is about kindling the pupils' imagination by the way that you present ideas. The way that you do this is as important as what you do. Your whole manner — your voice, tone, facial expression and the level of interest that you signify can help you get a lesson off to a good start. Miss Gibbs did not signal to the pupils that she was interested in railways, the topic that she was trying to teach, or in them individually or as a group. They felt that she was trying to keep them occupied and reacted accordingly. Their only real interest was either in deciding the minimum they could do in order to get by, or in winding up the teacher.

Miss Gibbs had failed to enthuse her pupils about the topic she was trying to teach, so how should you set about it? What kind of approach should you take?

There is no clear agreement about the best manner to adopt in the classroom, just as there is no blueprint for successful teaching. Different approaches work for different people. The case study below illustrates this point.

CASE STUDY 6.2. FOR ACTION

The Science Lesson

The class arrives. They pause at the teacher's bench, where the equipment is set up. 'What's that for, Miss?', they ask. 'What are we doing today?' The questions are good humoured, interested and they all gather round the bench, but Mrs Berry tells them sharply to go to their places, sit down and get their exercise books out. When they have all arrived, she greets them formally and takes the register, stopping occasionally to insist on silence. Then she tells them to copy the title from the whiteboard and to come forward to watch her carry out the experiment. There is some chat as they move and she quells this and tells them where to stand so that they can see the experiment clearly. In fact these positions also help her to keep an eye on the class during the experiment and to control it. 'Tim, you stand there, Gwen and Anne, over there,' she says. There is some muttering, but they know it is no good to argue with Mrs Berry.

She begins the demonstration. She is very crisp and lucid in her delivery and they can all see what she is doing. She uses the technical term and then defines it in simpler terms for them. She repeats the point before going on to the next step and does this without losing pace. She is regarded as a very competent teacher and this shows in the demonstration – the pupils watch fascinated. The room is completely and attentively silent, except for the sound of the teacher's voice. Individual pupils nod occasionally. At one stage Reshma asks, 'Why did it do that?' Mrs Berry gives her a clear succinct explanation and Reshma nods, 'Yes, I can see now,' she says. 'Good', says Mrs Berry, 'Let's continue.'

Having completed the experiment, Mrs Berry tells the pupils to return to their places. Then she gives them some notes about how the experiment was conducted, what chemical changes took place and what the experiment proved. She speaks at the right speed for the class, spells difficult or technical words onto a section of the board prepared for this activity and her diction is very clear. It is rare for a pupil to ask her to repeat a phrase or a sentence. Finally the class copy a diagram of the experiment from the whiteboard. Homework is to learn their work for an end-of-module test in a week's time. The class leave more quietly than they arrived. Anne is heard saying to Gwen, 'That was really interesting. I liked seeing the way the colours changed in that experiment.'

For action/discussion:

What approach to teaching did Mrs Berry take and how effective was it?
How did the pupils regard her and why?
In what respects did she communicate successfully with the class?
What opportunities were missed?

For action:

Rewrite this case study using a totally different teaching style.

For reflection:
What demands were made on the pupils during this lesson?
The lesson described above was a traditional, chalk-and-talk lesson which included a demonstration of a chemistry experiment. The style adopted by the teacher was both authoritarian and didactic. In this lesson:

She instructed the pupils what to do – they obeyed her orders.
She carried out the experiment – they watched.
She described and explained the experiment – they listened.
She dictated the notes – they wrote down what she said.
She drew the diagram onto the board – they copied it.
She talked – they were silent; attempts to chat were quelled.
She proved the hypothesis – they recorded the result.
She transmitted information – they received it.

Within the limits Mrs Berry set herself, this was a very successful lesson. It was well taught and the teacher communicated with the pupils effectively. Her exposition was extremely lucid; it held the pupils' attention, they accepted that this teacher knew what she was doing and, in stark contrast to the previous case study, the pupils' expectation of this lesson was high. They expected the demonstration to be good and that the experiment would work. She got the pace exactly right – it was neither too fast nor too slow. Her explanations were succinct and clear. The language she used matched the group: she was neither condescending nor too demanding. The correct technical terms were used, but always explained, and if a pupil said, 'I don't understand,' or 'How does that work?' she explained simply and clearly and summarized and reinforced well.

The skills demanded from the pupils, however, were not high-level skills and the pupils' role was largely passive. The skills were:

- listening
- simple comprehension
- accurate copying from the board or dictation
- recall, regurgitation of information.

The experiment generated the pupils' interest, but no demands were made on their creativity or imaginations. It is an extreme example of a teacher seeing her role as a transmitter of information – telling the pupils what to think or believe, demonstrating how something works, providing information which they can learn and reproduce and testing to see how well the knowledge has been transmitted and assimilated.

Explaining

Much of what you have to teach depends on how well you explain it to the pupils. The case study about the chemistry lesson illustrated this point. The teacher explained the ideas successfully through her demonstration and through verbal explanation, and the two methods complemented each other. Most explanation, however, comes through teacher talk – describing, giving information, exposition, illustration and interpretation. Sometimes it is built up through question and answer. It is not enough to understand the topic yourself, it has to be delivered at the level of the pupils' understanding. In the chemistry lesson in the case study, Mrs Berry got this exactly right. Beginner teachers often find it difficult to judge the level of pupil understanding correctly, expect more background knowledge than the pupils are likely to have, and use language that is too technical, too difficult or too consciously condescending for the pupils to tolerate. So the first step should be to consider the ages of the pupils, your assessment of their abilities and their previous knowledge of the topic.

CASE STUDY 6.3. FOR REFLECTION

(To be used in conjunction with case study 6.2.)
There are obviously many forms and levels of explanation, but whatever the topic or idea to be explained, there are some common principles around which you should plan your exposition. Brown and Armstrong (1984) identify five basic skills:

- clarity and fluency – defining new terms clearly and appropriate use of explicit language
- emphasis and interest – making good use of voice, gestures, materials and paraphrasing
- using examples – appropriate in type and quality
- organization – presence of a logical sequence and use of link words and phrases
- feedback – offering a chance for pupils to ask questions and assess learning outcomes.

How Many of these Skills did Mrs Berry Demonstrate in the Chemistry Lesson?

Clarity and fluency were evident throughout the lesson

She easily passed the language test:

- she was extremely clear and lucid
- she was precise, avoiding vagueness of speech
- she used technical terms where they fitted, but always explained their meaning to the pupils
- she was careful to use language which matched the ability levels of this mixed ability group, ie repeating the point using different words and phrases to describe the same thing where this facilitated understanding.

Emphasis and interest

- her voice and tone kept interest throughout the lesson through their authority and clarity
- she paced the lesson well – she did not go too quickly for the slower pupils, nor did the more able become bored. The lesson progressed at a satisfactory pace and she managed to speak, including dictation, at a speed and pitch which suited the pupils
- the demonstration excited interest. The pupils wanted to see the experiment, so they concentrated.

Using examples

The case study does not mention that Mrs Berry used examples, though the demonstration could be counted as one way of showing the pupils how a system or idea worked in practice. Where examples are used, they work best if they come from the pupils' experience, otherwise they just confuse the issue. Appropriate use of lively detail can help to put flesh on the bare bones of an idea. Be careful, however, not to lose sight of your learning objective either through using too much detail or because the example leads you into a side-track.

Organization

The lesson was very well organized:

- it was developed logically, with a clear sequence and good links, so that the pupils understood what was happening and what was expected of them
- she organized her board well, eg a section was set aside for spellings. This was an established procedure and the pupils knew what to expect.

Feedback

Mrs Berry clearly summarized and reinforced well, largely by repeating points using different words, or when, for example, Reshma said that she did not understand, by providing additional explanation. However, because she was essentially a transmitter, this teacher did not involve the pupils in formulating the explanation. A useful technique which provides quick feedback can be to get the pupils to explain some of the aspects of what they have seen or to represent it in diagrammatic form. Mrs Berry played safe, dictated the notes, and drew the diagram onto the board for the pupils to copy. They seem to have coped, but she was having to use a formal test to check what they had learnt from the lesson.

If the Pupils Have Not Understood the Explanation

If the pupils don't seem to grasp it the first time, it is no real use to keep repeating the same message unchanged, as there is something wrong with either the message itself, or your method of relaying it. Failure to understand may occur for a number of reasons, for example:

■   you haven't taken account of the pupils' level of mental development, eg you are using language which is above their heads
■   you have failed to engage their interest – the pupils haven't listened
■   you have included too much detail or too many ideas and confused the pupils
■   your explanation was too imprecise and the pupils could not grasp what it was about.

What this adds up to is that you haven't thought it through sufficiently well. The checklist of dos and don'ts which follows is intended to help you plan and prepare.

A Checklist of Dos and Don'ts

1.   Don't just lecture – you will bore the pupils and lose their attention
2.   Don't go on for too long – for the same reasons as no.1. You will quickly find that the children's attention span is relatively short. Whatever their ability level, 20 minutes is the absolute limit for exposition.

3. Keep it simple – the more complicated it becomes, the harder it is to follow an explanation. Try not to introduce too many ideas at the same time; most people can only cope with one new concept at a time.
4. Remember to define new or technical terms and to check that difficult words are understood.
5. Use variations in your voice and gestures to encourage interest and understanding.
6. Think about whether visual aids, diagrams or practical demonstrations would be better than words. Avoid only using instruction sheets – include verbal instructions as well.
7. Make sure that you match the pace and language to the needs of the group.
8. Be patient – avoid sounding irritated if you have to repeat or clarify. Try hard to avoid saying, 'I've explained that once already.'
9. Beware of assuming that your listeners are either stupid or wildly enthusiastic about what is being offered to them – your explanation will have to capture their attention.
10. Check that they have understood. Remember to use repetition and paraphrasing. If your explanation seems unsuccessful – pupils are confused or repeatedly fail to grasp the point – be prepared to think again about your approach to the topic.

CASE STUDY 6.4 FOR ACTION

Explaining about locks

It was a rainy Thursday afternoon and Miss Gibbs was not looking forward to her session with 9G. The Industrial Revolution at Key Stage 3 did not seem to interest this class at all and both teacher and pupils found it heavy going. Barbara Gibbs was a very conscientious teacher, however, so she persevered. Today the topic was canals, and she was endeavouring to explain to the class the principles on which the first canals were built and how locks had to be constructed in order to raise or lower the water level. She did not find such a technical subject at all easy to explain, but she did her best. She tried to describe as simply as she could why locks were needed and how they worked. 9G was not the most intelligent of groups, and there was no point using too difficult language, but never the less they seemed totally unable to grasp it. The more she repeated the information, the more confused they seemed to become. She was not certain whether some members of the class were trying to wind her up. When Billy Wiltshire said, yet again, 'I don't understand, Miss, why does the water go up?' her patience snapped and she almost screamed at him, 'I've explained that several times already, Billy, and I'm not going to repeat it again.'

For action/discussion:

What was the problem with this lesson and how could Miss Gibbs improve her communication with this class?

Questioning

Questions play a very important part in most lessons. It has been suggested that teachers in any week ask more than 1,000 questions – this is something like one per minute. Whether or not you ask as many questions as this, it is clear that to be effective in the classroom, you will have to develop your skills in asking questions. It is particularly relevant to you as a new teacher because research has shown that NQTs tend to ask fewer questions than experienced teachers, perhaps because they fear that managing pupil response could generate class control problems.

Why Do Teachers Ask So Many Questions?

Teachers talk a great deal, some as much as 60 per cent of the time. Questions provide an opportunity for the pupils to participate in the lesson – to talk back, to show what they have understood or learnt and to contribute ideas.

CASE STUDY 6.5. FOR REFLECTION

Brown and Edmondson (1984) have compiled a list of reasons given by teachers for asking questions. It is extremely comprehensive and could be useful for you to reflect on it and compare it with your own practice. The reasons are given in order of frequency of use:

■ to encourage thought, understanding of ideas, phenomena, procedures and values
■ to check understanding, knowledge and skills

- to gain attention to task, to enable the teacher to move towards teaching points, as a warm up activity for pupils
- to review, revise, recall or reinforce a recently learned point, to remind the pupils of earlier procedures
- to teach the whole class through pupil answers
- to give everyone a chance to answer
- to draw in shy pupils
- to probe pupils' knowledge after critical answers
- to allow expression of feelings, views and empathy.

For action/discussion:

Discuss this list with your mentor and get him/her to monitor a lesson and see how your questioning style compares with this list. It could also be useful for both of you if you followed up this exercise by watching your mentor teach a lesson and this time round, you monitor how the questions are asked, and then you can compare the results. You could also do this exercise with a colleague in the department.

What Kind of Questions Do They Ask?

Most classroom questions are designed to check recall of factual information or to assess whether other kinds of learning have taken place. Research projects on teachers' questioning tend to support this assertion. One such project was undertaken by Trevor Kerry as part of the DES Teacher Education Project. It surveyed 32 lessons conducted by eight teachers and found that:

- over 80 per cent of the questions were of a lower order
- 15 per cent were concerned with classroom management, control or administration
- only about 5 per cent were higher-order questions.

The findings are discussed in Kerry's book, *Effective Questioning* (1982), together with some very helpful ideas and advice about how to improve your questioning; the suggestions, which are still valid, inform this chapter. More recent studies complement these findings, for example a study of RS teaching found that out of 400 questions, 79 per cent were lower-order.

Questions are usually divided into two types: open or closed, and higher- or lower-order.

A *closed* question will require a monosyllabic or single correct answer, eg, 'When did the battle of Hastings take place?' The answer: 7 October 1066, is either right or wrong and demands simple recall of historical data.

An *open* question will have more than one right answer. An open question, eg, 'Why do you think the Normans defeated the Saxons in 1066?' can be answered with reference to the strengths of the Normans or the weakness of the Saxons. It can highlight weapons or strategies used by either army or the personal qualities of the leaders. It is unlikely that only one of these factors produced the Norman victory and historians would differ as to which factor they considered to be the most important. This question would encourage pupils to speculate, to offer ideas and assess possibilities.

The first example, 'When did the battle of Hastings take place?', would be considered a *lower-order* question. To answer it the pupil simply supplies the date. Lower-order questions test recall or simple comprehension, eg, 'Can you give me another example of....'

The second example, 'Why do you think that the Normans defeated the Saxons in 1066?' is a *higher-order* question because it encourages the pupils to think. To answer it well the pupils have to demonstrate a good level of historical skills. They have to understand that an event can have more than one cause; that some causes may be more important than others; and that causes may be linked and can interact. It involves not only the generation of ideas, but reasoning, analysis and evaluation, and is therefore much more demanding than the first question.

Open questions draw out the pupils and encourage them to contribute. Such questions often start, 'Why ...?', or 'What did you notice about ...?', or 'How would you do it?' The 'Why' questions encourage the pupils to reason; the 'What did you notice?' questions make them active watchers or readers and invite them to respond. 'How' questions, although open because they seek an explanation, can be lower-order questions if they merely demand a simple explanation of how something works, but they test observation and the ability of the pupil to explain and, if used well, they can provide the opportunity to speculate about a complex system. 'How would you do it?' invites the pupils to problem-solve by offering their own ideas.

CASE STUDY 6.8. FOR REFLECTION/ACTION

Kerry (op cit.) has produced a detailed analysis of questions and divided them into nine types. Question types 1-5 are more closed than types 6-9; 1-5 demand shorter answers, less thought and little competence in the language used by the pupils, whereas types 6-9 are much more demanding.

Types of Question

1. A data recall question - requires the pupil to remember facts or information without putting the information to use, eg, 'What are the four rules of number?'
2. A naming question - asks the pupil simply to name an event, process, phenomenon, etc. without showing insight into how the event, etc. is linked to other factors, eg, 'What do we call the set of bones covering the lungs?'
3. An observation question - asks the pupils to describe what they see without attempting to explain it, eg, 'What happened when we added litmus solution to hydrochloric acid?'
4. A control question - involves the use of questions to modify pupils' behaviour, eg, 'Will you sit down, John?'
5. A pseudo question - is constructed to appear that the teacher will accept more than one response, but in fact s/he has clearly made up his/her mind that this is not so, eg, 'Do you feel that beating slaves was a good thing, then?'
6. A speculative or hypothesis-generating question - asks the pupils to speculate about the outcome of a hypothetical situation, eg, 'Imagine a world without trees, how would this affect our lives?'
7. A reasoning or analysis question - asks the pupils to give reasons why certain things do or do not happen, eg, 'What motivates some young people to get involved in soccer violence?'
8. An evaluation question - is one which makes the pupil weigh up the pros and cons of a situation or argument, eg, 'How much evidence is there for the existence of an afterlife?'
9. A problem-solving question - asks pupils to construct ways of finding out answers to questions, eg, 'Suppose we wanted to discover what prompts birds to migrate, how do we go about it?'

For reflection/discussion:

Study this list and compare it with your own classroom practice. Think about why you have asked questions, where they have come in a lesson, whether they follow in a sequence and in what way the sequence built up. Look particularly at the proportion of open – closed, higher-order – lower-order questions that you ask. To help you analyse your practice, you may wish your mentor, or a colleague, to observe a lesson and record the questions, or even video a section of the lesson. Discuss your findings with your mentor, and suggest ways of improving your questioning.

If you do find that the majority of your questions are lower-level, this is not necessarily a disaster, nor does it make you a bad teacher. What you want to watch is that you don't omit higher-order questions altogether, and it may be useful for you to think about how you could increase the proportion of higher level questions that you use. What is really important, however, is to use the questions appropriately and effectively – they are a tool, not an end in themselves. Quite frequently, especially at the beginning of a lesson, you will want to recap on previous material in order to set the scene. You will not want to re-enact the whole of a previous discussion, and some fairly closed, short-answer questions are a suitable and effective technique to achieve this objective. A run of short-answer questions can help to build up understanding, whereas a difficult or complex question posed too soon in a lesson could result in confusion or silence. Good questioning often runs in sequence from lower- to higher-order, making progressively more demands on the pupils' thinking. They are also much more time-consuming. Answering a complicated higher-order question could occupy a large part of a lesson and this in itself is a limiting factor. You also want to make sure that you achieve your learning objective and are not side-tracked. Thus when you monitor your questioning in the way suggested in the case study above, it could be useful to discuss where in the lesson it would be most effective to include some higher-order questions. Case study 6.7 examines the way one teacher used questions as the basis for a discussion lesson.

CASE STUDY 6.7. FOR REFLECTION

Pupil Response

'What choices did King Louis XVI have in 1789 when the Third Estate occupied the Tennis Courts and declared itself the National Assembly?' Mrs Holden, who had sought to provoke a discussion with her Year 8 class, groaned inwardly when Katie's hand shot up immediately. Other hands, which had tentatively started to go up, sank back again. Mrs Holden suspected that, faced with Katie's enthusiasm to volunteer for anything and everything, the class had decided to let her do all the work. 'He could get the guards to deal with them,' suggested Katie. 'What, do you mean shoot them all?' inquired Mrs Holden. This response provoked some laughter, and Katie looked abashed. 'Surely they would only have to shoot a few of them to get the situation under control,' said William, drawn into the discussion despite himself. 'Well, that's one solution,' said Mrs Holden. 'Would someone like to come out and write all the suggestions onto the board so that we can all see them and think about them?' Katie's hand shot up at once, but this time Mrs Holden shook her head, 'You did it last time, Katie, it's time someone else had a turn. What about you, Mira?' she said to a very quiet girl at the end corner of the rectangle of tables in which this classroom was arranged. 'Will you write the ideas onto the board for us? ' Mira nodded, and came out to the front.

Mrs Holden then recapped: 'So far you have suggested that King Louis should use force against the representatives of the Third Estate, and that they should shoot a few of them in order to gain control. What do you think of this idea?' 'Wouldn't it make them even more angry?' asked Alice. 'Yes, it could make them very angry indeed,' said Mrs Holden, 'And what might the consequences of that be?' 'They might get reinforcements and fight the King,' said Trevor. 'Yes, something like that could have happened,' agreed Mrs Holden. 'It was possible that shooting some people could have restored order at the time but lead to a lot more trouble later. Do you think that using the guards in this way would be a good idea?' 'No,' said Rajesh emphatically, 'I think it would be a very bad idea, Louis should talk to them.' 'That's a very interesting suggestion, Rajesh, and quite different from Katie's,' said Mrs Holden. 'You think he should negotiate with the Third Estate?' 'Yes,' said Rajesh, 'If he listened to what they had to say he might be able to sort it all out.' 'That's a very sensible suggestion and one that, in his position, I might want to use,' commented Mrs Holden. 'If 8B went on a sit-down strike in the classroom because you were fed up or we had had a disagreement, this is the kind of approach I would adopt. I would talk to you, discuss the problem with you and try to sort it out, but how realistic a proposition is this when we apply it to King Louis XVI?' Now a lot of hands waved, and Mrs Holden selected a girl on the far right of the rectangle. 'It's not realistic, Louis couldn't have done it,' said Anna. 'What makes you think that?' Mrs Holden probed gently. 'Because he was a very weak King,' said Anna. 'He would have made a real mess of it.' 'Good!' said Mrs Holden, 'Now, can anyone think of another reason why negotiations would not have succeeded? What about you, Warren?' There was a pause while Warren thought, and Mrs Holden waited, ignoring other hands, then Warren said hesitantly, 'I don't think Louis understood why they were so angry, so he wouldn't have had anything to talk to them about.' 'That's a very good point Warren has made,' said Mrs Holden, 'Anna and Warren have suggested that Louis would not have been able to talk to the Third Estate because his understanding of the situation was very poor and he lacked the skill to negotiate successfully.' 'He wouldn't have wanted to lower the taxes, so he didn't have anything to offer them, did he?' interjected Lucy. 'But he might have gained time,' argued William. 'Time for what?' asked Alice. 'To get help,' said Katie. 'To send in the guards, you mean!' said William.

Mrs Holden intervened before this discussion could become acrimonious, and steered it firmly back on course: 'We've already agreed that negotiations might fail, so what options remain for Louis? Try to put yourself in his place.' 'I'd give up!' said Denise. 'The situation is too difficult for Louis to deal with.' 'Do you mean that he would abdicate?' asked Mrs Holden. 'What does abdicate mean?' asked Denise. 'Can anyone tell Denise? Eva, do you know?' 'Abdicate means stopping being King or Queen,' answered Eva. 'That's right,' said Mrs Holden, 'Now, what do you think about that as an idea?' Several of the class nodded their agreement with this suggestion. 'I can see that a lot of you think it is a good idea,' she said, 'and that the answer for Louis is to stop being King, but what would happen to him then?' 'They would probably kill him,' said William, rubbing his hands together. 'You are clearly relishing the idea,' said Mrs Holden, smiling at him. 'Are you sure he would abdicate if it meant putting his life at risk?' Now they shook their heads, but Denise said, 'He could run away.' 'Where to?' interjected Katie. 'To his brother-in-law of course. Don't you remember, Marie Antoinette's brother was the Emperor of Austria,' said Lucy crushingly, pleased to be able to squash Katie. 'He'd be safe there.' 'Good thinking,' said Mrs Holden, 'though you've gone ahead of events a bit. This did happen, but not in 1789. Things had not yet reached so critical a point that Louis decided to flee from France.' 'So what was there left for Louis to do?' asked Richard. 'Look at the board, where Mira has managed to put up all your suggestions while you were arguing. Well done, Mira!' said the teacher.

'We have had a lot of good ideas,' she continued, 'but it was none of the things we have said so far, and it is time that we rounded it up.' 'Will you tell us?' asked Ruth. 'Let us have one last guess before I tell you what happened.' Mrs Holden replied. 'Lucy, you have had a lot of good ideas this lesson, what do you think really happened?' Lucy thought for a moment, 'Well,' she said, ' Louis was so weak and stupid that he probably just gave in and let them tell him what to do next.' 'Well done, Lucy!' said Mrs Holden, 'That's spot on. On July 9th Louis gave in and ordered the other two estates to join the Third Estate. You are quite right because that meant that he had lost control of the situation. Now, for homework ...'

For action:
Analyse the questions against the list of nine types given earlier in this chapter.

What proportion of the questions were open, higher-level, closed, lower-level, administrative?
What techniques did she use to involve pupils?
How did she respond to their answers?
How did Mrs Holden handle Katie – what techniques did she use and with what success?

In this case study the teacher ran a class discussion largely through the use of questions. This technique is used frequently in subjects such as history. To use it effectively, considerable skill is needed. In the case study above the teacher was both experienced and effective. She proved skilful at getting the pupils to participate in spite of their initial reluctance, and in moving the discussion forward. How did she manage to do this?

■ She used a lot of open questions such as 'What do you think about...?' which made pupils think, reflect and offer suggestions.
■ She used some administrative questions: 'Will someone write the ideas on the board?' instead of giving an instruction, or to check: 'Have you got all that, Mira?'
■ She checked definitions; 'Can anyone tell Denise what abdicate means?'
■ She used pupils' names – this helped her to draw pupils into the discussion.
■ She addressed some questions to the whole class. Often these were used as starter questions where a range of suggestions could be made and discussed and the order did not matter. Sometimes she picked up on several nods of agreement as indicating general assent.
■ She targeted some questions at particular pupils. This allowed her to select the level of difficulty. For example a

very able and perceptive pupil was asked the final question because a specific high-level answer was required. She wanted to draw the discussion to a conclusion by getting a pupil to supply the historically correct solution. This was risky, so she chose the pupil most likely to succeed. She also gave herself a let-out by saying, 'If Lucy cannot do it, then I'll tell you.'

■ She used a room arrangement in which pupils faced each other – this encouraged participation.

■ She directed questions around the room to areas where research has indicated that you might not expect the highest level of involvement (such as the far right of the rectangle).

■ She involved a very quiet pupil by making her the scribe.

■ She regularly summarized where the discussion had reached, then she moved the discussion forward by asking the next question. She was checking and reinforcing understanding and providing a clear framework to a complex set of questions. In another lesson she might have asked a pupil to summarize; here it could have defeated her purpose.

■ Not all the questions were asked by the teacher, some were asked by pupils. This gave them ownership of the discussion, which was teacher-controlled but not teacher-dominated. It enabled discussion between pupils, yet when it began to disintegrate, she brought it firmly back on course.

■ Each option was fully discussed and assessed before moving on to the next. Serious consideration was given to each idea offered and suggestions were never dismissed as frivolous.

■ Her responses to pupils were positive and encouraged them without being over fulsome. Most of the time she simply said, 'Yes', often she said, 'Good' and she used such phrases as 'That's an interesting idea', or 'That's a very sensible suggestion.' To get Warren to speak, she waited, 'ignoring other hands ... ' and then applauded his suggestion. When Lucy got the difficult final question right, Mrs Holden was appreciative and exclaimed, 'That's spot on, well done Lucy!'

She reacted negatively to one pupil only – Katie, and this was to limit the damage that this pupil's desire to hog attention and answer every question was doing to a class discussion. Her answers and the manner she used towards Katie gave signals to the class. She allowed Katie to answer the first question, but put her down, though not cruelly. She did not say, 'Nonsense, what a stupid idea!' rather, she exaggerated Katie's answer and made it sound more extreme than it really was; some pupils laughed and

Katie was abashed. Squashing Katie encouraged others to respond. Then she refused to accept Katie as board scribe, making it clear to the class that Katie had had her turn in a previous lesson. Choosing a pupil who never volunteered also gave signals to the class. In this way she gradually drew a lot of pupils into the discussion.

Effective Classroom Speaking

Earlier in the chapter we noted that you could be speaking for as much as 60 per cent of your time in the classroom. This makes how you use your voice a very important factor in delivering a lesson successfully – how you say something may be as important as what you have to say.

Some Hints for Effective Classroom Speaking

- Aim for a firm natural voice – with a hint of authority.
- A voice with a natural low pitch is easier to listen to than a high-pitched voice and can sound more authoritative.
- Emphasize key words or phrases in the exposition so that pupils can recognize and understand them.
- Vary your voice to suit different circumstances – a continuously monotonous voice can be tedious to listen to.
- Try to avoid developing exaggerated mannerisms – you're not sending semaphore.
- Try to develop the use of slight pauses to highlight important points and key words.
- In a large room you may need to speak more slowly in order to be heard.
- Never simply assume that all the pupils have heard – watch them to check this.
- In a hall, direct your voice to the back row.
- Try not to let your voice die away at the end of sentences, for example by dropping your voice as you look down at your notes.
- Check the pronunciation of difficult, technical or unusual words beforehand so that you do not sound nervous or uncertain of yourself.
- A higher standard of speech is necessary in the classroom than that which is required in everyday conversation. This is because you must set an example. Try to be grammatically

correct, otherwise you will lose the pupils' respect. Avoid saying 'Ok', 'Right', 'All right' and using slang.

CASE STUDY 6.8. FOR ACTION/DISCUSSION

I am sure that the new English teacher does know the set books, but Jane cannot understand her because of her accent.

Mrs Gatlin, headteacher at Bestwick Park High School, has received a letter about a new teacher. Her first step in dealing with it is to discuss it with the mentor as she will want the mentor to deal with the matter and report back to her.

The NQT, Helen, is an American with a pronounced transatlantic twang, but neither the head nor the mentor found it at all difficult to understand her. A new or unfamiliar voice can constitute a problem, but usually this is temporary as the class adapts to the teacher and begins to recognize and understand her voice and mannerisms, so that the mentor had to consider whether something else was causing this problem. Criticisms of something minor such as a teacher's accent might be a way of flagging up a more serious concern. For this reason the best way forward seemed to be for the mentor to go to a lesson with the class concerned and observe the interaction between the teacher and the pupils. Observing a lesson clarified the position. The class was restless and fidgety. Their concentration level was low. Teacher input was quite lengthy and there was little interaction between teacher and pupils. When Helen did ask a question, the pupils tended not to respond or to say that they did not understand. Watching the pupils made it clear to the mentor that they had turned off from this lesson. The problem lay with Helen's voice and approach, but not with her accent. She droned and went on for too long – the pupils found her dull and had turned off.

For action/discussion:

You are Helen's mentor – how would you tackle this problem?
What advice would you give Helen?
What can Helen do to improve her relationship with this group?

The case study above mainly centred on the teacher's voice, but criticisms of something minor are often a way of raising a more serious problem, for example the relationship between the class and its new teacher has not gelled, or the class don't accept the competence of the teacher.

In this case there is a hint in the letter that the writer is doubtful about the teacher's competence, so the mentor had to check that the voice problem was not just the tip of an iceberg.

Not Using Your Voice

How Much Does Body Language Matter?

It is not just the words you use or how you use your voice that affects the success of your lesson: your body language is also important. Movement, gestures, mannerisms and eye contact all contribute to effective class control and good teaching. Indeed public relations consultants have pointed out that nine-tenths of a speaker's impact depends on his/her appearance and only one-tenth on what s/he actually says.

To be an effective teacher you will need the right image, as you have to convey confidence and competence to the classes which you teach. You will want to convey an image that the pupils recognize as authoritative, competent, alert and firm yet sympathetic, but this is not at all easy to achieve. All too frequently new teachers are so concerned about getting the content of their lessons right, because this is so important to their credibility, that they give little thought to how they look and what messages they are giving to the class. Trainee or new teachers often look and sound tense or nervous — a worried expression gives out a signal to the pupils that in some way this person is unsure of him/herself. Older, secondary pupils are particularly good at appreciating the teacher's underlying mood and if they start to suspect your apprehension, then all the effort you have put into getting the content right could be wasted because they will begin to question your authority. The problem is that you will probably be unaware that this is happening — so how can you avoid it?

Just as public figures, especially politicians, learn to adapt their appearance and body language in order to improve their general performance, so it could be very worth your while at least to assess the impact that you are making in the classroom and to think about how you could improve your image as a teacher. To do this you may want some help from a colleague or your mentor, who will need to observe some lessons and record your mannerisms. The list of dos and don'ts given below can serve as guidelines for the observation; it is not of course a blueprint for success. Much will depend upon your own personality and how you interpret the advice – do not use it too rigidly, but try to pick from the menu of suggestions ideas which could improve your classroom technique. It is most likely that you will find that you need to be more visibly assertive in your body language, but it could be the case that your presence is too overpowering, it is preventing the pupils from learning effectively and you would teach better if you were less dominant in the classroom.

Some Dos and Don'ts

Movement

One thing that you can do is to give some thought to how you stand and move. Try to make your movements purposeful, calm and unhurried. An effective teacher conveys the impression that s/he is a force to be reckoned with and this effect partly depends on how s/he looks and stands. Sometimes you will hear this called 'having presence'.

Some things to avoid:

- shifting your weight from one foot to another – the class will watch your feet!
- fiddling with your clothing or jewellery – it indicates nervousness and distracts attention
- grasping your lapels – this appears pompous
- glancing at your watch – this suggests that you are desperate for the end of the lesson to come
- jerky or hurried movements – they are another indicator of nervousness
- drooping – standing straight gives a much more positive impression
- sitting down too much – effective teachers tend to spend most of the lesson on their feet. Whole-class teaching and exposition work best this way, and even while the pupils are working, it is advisable to get up from time to time and walk round the room: it shows that you are alert and in charge
- striding around with your hands on your hips – this can seem intimidating
- hovering over pupils – this can be quite threatening. It is better to sit or crouch beside a pupil to help him/her individually.

Gestures

Gestures and positive facial expressions will reinforce your control. You may find it helpful to exaggerate gestures a bit – remember that to some extent you are centre stage and giving a performance. This means that it is OK for your gestures to be more pronounced than in ordinary conversation, though be careful not to overdo it or you will find pupils giving imitations of you or inventing unflattering nicknames for you, which could take years to live down. Women tend to use gestures more frequently than men, so male teachers should beware of being too static in the classroom and women of over-indulgence in gestures. Accompanying the gestures with a smile or a frown will make all the difference to how they are interpreted.

Some ways of using your hands:

- using your fingers to count or indicate important points reinforces ideas
- holding your hand up with the palm upwards indicates that you have information to offer
- holding an unseen object with both hands indicates you have an idea to present
- pointing can be used positively or negatively; it is probably the gesture most commonly used in teaching
- a wave of the hand can encourage or dismiss a suggestion
- hand-chopping through the air usually adds vehemence as you emphasize points that matter; chopping sideways can indicate that something is incorrect
- leaning forward can indicate interest
- leaning on your hands usually adds intensity to what you are saying
- wagging your finger at a pupil tends to indicate mild disapproval; it is also sometimes used for emphasis.

Some things to avoid:

- waving your arms around like a windmill – this is very distracting and confusing
- sitting womb-like with your arms folded tightly around you – this conveys your tension and anxiety and signals 'Keep out'
- gestures made only from the elbow – they look feeble and stilted; always make gestures from the shoulder
- pointing directly at a pupil can be very threatening – make sure that you mean to do this

- running your hands through your hair – indicates that the situation is getting out of control and you don't know what to do about it
- putting your head in your hands – use very rarely to indicate horror, despair or 'How on earth did this happen!'

At all costs avoid touching pupils. Touching is a very powerful means of communication, but nowadays it could lead to such serious problems for you that the best advice we can offer you is not to touch pupils at all. For primary teachers and PE teachers, where touch is almost essential to the job, specialist advice may be needed.

Eye contact

Eye contact is one of the most important techniques to get right. A direct gaze with your eyes repeatedly scanning the room indicates to the pupils that you are alert and in charge. Gazing directly at a child answering a question indicates your interest in his/her answer. Gazing directly at a child who is not concentrating indicates that you have noticed the inattention and expect the pupil to do something about it.

Good teachers raise their eyebrows a lot to give out a variety of messages. Raising your eyebrows expresses surprise – you have noticed something or did not expect something. Accompanied with a smile it condones or encourages. More often it is accompanied by a frown as it is one of the most well-known first indicators of a teacher's disapproval. If it is ineffective it is likely to be followed by a verbal reprimand. It can of course be combined with other gestures.

If you have glasses, looking over them at a pupil or pupils can be very effective, but it must be done with panache or you will become one of the school's unsuccessful eccentrics. Practice this technique before you use it regularly.

Avoid not looking directly at the class or pupil to whom you are talking. This will be interpreted as weakness or that you can't cope with the situation. If it is difficult or embarrassing to look directly at the pupil, at least focus in the general direction and upwards, perhaps to a point slightly above his/her head. Looking at your feet or away from the pupil gives a very negative impression

Be aware, however, that cultural differences can affect whether a pupil will look directly at you and only castigate a pupil who cannot meet your eyes if it is appropriate to do so.

Facial expression

Smiling, frowning or standing poker-faced, you make an impression on the class — your expression encourages or deters. Lack of expression suggests lack of interest or that you do not consider the class or the topic to be important. The expression you ought to use most is your smile; most new teachers don't smile enough. Obviously you want to asset your control and be firm, but your smile is an asset which you should exploit. It encourages pupils, draws them in and helps to make the lesson a positive experience for them.

Do not be afraid to lead the laughter when something funny happens. If you lead it, you can establish when the laughter should stop so that it will not get out of control. It also means that the pupils laugh with you and not at you.

A rebuke or correction said with a smile indicates to the pupil that it is not the end of the world and can help to make the criticism more acceptable.

Some things to avoid:

- frequent meaningless or shrill laughter – this is like a nervous cough or tic: it indicates anxiety and makes the pupils suspect that you are not in control
- failure to smile combined with a constant worried expression – another indicator of anxiety which does not inspire confidence.

Listening

Teachers often grumble that pupils do not listen, but a very important stimulus to pupils is the teacher's own example. Listening is a vital communication skill. Listening to pupils with total and undivided attention is one of the most effective ways of showing them that they are valued. It indicates to them that you are taking them seriously, and makes them feel that they matter. In this way it helps them to develop a positive self-image. You are communicating that what they have to say is relevant and is a serious contribution to the lesson. Listening to what the pupils say will also help you to understand them better — to appreciate how they perceive things and what their attitudes and feelings are.

This is not a recipe for listening to gossip or indeed gossiping with pupils which will do your image no good at all; rather it means taking notice of their contributions to discussion and valuing them. In case study 6.6, Mrs Holden, the teacher, was a good listener. Each pupil's contribution to the discussion was seriously considered and assessed. Even when she rejected a suggestion, Mrs Holden smiled at and generally encouraged the pupil so that s/he would not feel rejected and would want to participate in future. She was also able to build on her good knowledge of the class.

For action:
Active listening obviously takes time, but it pays such good dividends that it is well worth the effort. A useful exercise could be for your mentor to observe a lesson for listening skills and to discuss where you stand on the spectrum and how you could enhance your skills.

CHAPTER 7

Marking and Assessment

What is Assessment?

To be an effective teacher you need to ensure that you achieve your lesson objectives. This means that the pupils should have learnt what you have tried to teach them, but how do you know whether they have learnt anything? Finding out what the pupils have learnt will involve you in assessment. It is how you evaluate what progress the pupils have made. You will want to know such things as:

- what the pupil has understood
- what skills the pupil has acquired
- where the pupil stands in relation to other pupils
- what the pupil knows now
- what the pupil has not understood
- where the gaps in learning are
- whether the pupil is ready to progress to the next stage in learning.

Assessment thus provides you with feedback about what and how much the pupils have learnt. Different kinds of assessment will give you different information about the pupils' progress. You can assess pupils in a whole variety of ways:

- through oral or written tasks
- by different criteria, eg, norm-referenced tests (the grading of a pupil's performance in relation to others) or criterion-referenced tests (whether the pupil has met the criteria)
- by self-assessment, peer assessment or teacher assessment
- through continuous assessment or formal end of term,

module or year tests
- through class tests or external examinations
- through formative/diagnostic assessment or summative/final assessment.

These methods are not mutually exclusive and you may find that in assessing the pupils you will need to employ more than one technique at the time.

Is Marking the Same as Assessment?

Marking is a form of assessment. It entails giving the pupils a grade or mark for a piece of work and usually some feedback about how the task was tackled. Any assignment, oral, written or practical, can be marked, but most of your time will be spent in evaluating the pupils' written work.

What is Expected of You?

Marking is one of the most time-consuming parts of a teacher's job and often one of the least enjoyable. It is frequently said that we spend more time marking work than preparing lessons and this could well be true. The following comment from a staff handbook illustrates the still widely held expectation that written tasks and their marking are central to teaching :

In addition to formal tests and examinations it is expected that every piece of written work a child produces will be marked and an assessment made of its worth.

This is a daunting prospect for any new teacher as you may find yourself with at least one class in each year group and two classes in some year groups. How can you be expected to cope with all this marking and how frequently do you have to do it? The answer to these questions depends on what you interpret as marking. If it is to write copiously on every book or file for every exercise undertaken, then indeed it is never-ending and you could well end up not only extremely tired, but with a problem in balancing the time you spend on marking against the time you need to spend preparing your lessons.

CASE STUDY 7.1. FOR REFLECTION/DISCUSSION

The list below is designed to make you reflect on ways through which you could approach marking; it is taken from Benton (1981). It was produced as a contribution to the Teacher Education Project and is as relevant today as when it was written.

What options are open to a teacher faced with thirty pieces of work ready for marking? S/he could:

- Go through each individual exercise meticulously correcting all errors including spelling, grammar and punctuation.
- Be selective in choosing particular errors eg 'This time I am going to mark for ...'
- Correct understanding or mistakes of content.
- Give a mark or a grade.
- Make a note in his/her mark book of particular problems.
- Suggest/require corrections to be done.
- Go over areas of common difficulty with the whole class.
- Read out particular pieces.
- See individual pupils about their work.
- 'Publish' the work in some way, eg place a copy on display.
- Simply put a tick to indicate it had been read.
- Use it as the basis for further work.

Discuss with your mentor the possible options so that you develop an acceptable pattern of marking. Of course not all the options given above are mutually exclusive and you may wish to employ a combination, or to use different approaches at different times. There is no one right approach, but your marking should match the context of the work. Indeed the best advice we could give you is that what matters most is that the students should know clearly not only what are the aims of the task which they are being set, but also how they are to be assessed. If it is spelt out to them at the outset that you will mark this assignment in a particular way, there will be fewer grumbles at the end of the topic when the books are returned. They will need to know what criteria you will use, how important you consider the assignment to be and whether they will be participating in the assessment.

One thing you might find helpful is to discuss with other teachers and then with your mentor how much time they spend on marking per week so that you get an idea of what a typical marking load is in your school and how other teachers cope. You may find some variation dependent upon subject, but a picture should emerge which will provide a guideline by which you can operate. Doing some of your marking in class is one way to cut down the burden of work to take home. It is also a useful opportunity to discuss with individual pupils how they are doing and to give advice, but if you do it too often the children begin to suspect that it is at the expense of new learning and this could affect your relationship with them, so it is important to get the balance right.

Nowadays it is likely that you will find that the school or the department already has a clear marking policy, in which case you must conform to its requirements. Below there is an example of one department's marking scheme. Use it as a point of comparison. It exists to help the teachers achieve a uniform approach and to help the pupils know where they stand.

CASE STUDY 7.2. EXEMPLAR AND FOR REFLECTION

Bestwick Park High School, Science Department Marking Policy Key Stage 3, Years 7–9

Work in exercise books should normally be marked using grades A–D. The criteria for these grades are similar to those used on the school reports, ie:

A = very good
B = good
C = just satisfactory
D = unsatisfactory.

This system should be explained to pupils at the beginning of the school year. The grade need not be an overall grade for a piece of work, but is often more useful if it is based upon a particular piece of work, eg, the clarity of a written description of an experimental method. It is important in this case that the pupils are quite clear about the criteria being used to grade their work. The grade may also be accompanied by a comment. Comments should usually offer constructive advice upon a pupil's work, and are often more helpful if they concentrate upon a particular aspect of a pupil's performance. The grade awarded should reflect the standard of written work as well as the scientific content of the assignment, and all errors in spelling and punctuation should be corrected.

Commendations for good work will be awarded to pupils achieving three A grades in their work, or to those who have produced an outstanding individual piece of work, or who have shown significant improvement.

Consistently poor work or repeated failure to hand in homework should be reported to the appropriate head of department.

Some Things to Avoid When Marking

- Making spelling or grammatical mistakes in your own comments – pupils and parents will seize on these as ammunition against you.
- Building up a backlog of unmarked work – this creates a bad impression as pupils begin to think you don't care and creates a problem for you as the backlog becomes unmanageable.
- Marking down a piece of work because a pupil misbehaved. Always keep behaviour separate from academic performance.
- Marking up or down because of your prior expectation of how a pupil will perform – this smells of favouritism.
- Too much red ink – it confuses the pupils, who can't work out which criticisms really matter.
- Only writing critical comments – it demotivates pupils.
- Engaging in altercations with pupils about the marks you have given their work.

What Should You Do About Spelling?

Correcting every spelling mistake is extremely time-consuming and covers the pupil's work in red ink, so what line should you take? Spelling seems to matter much more to some teachers than others and this seems to depend on personality and general approach rather than whether they teach English or other subjects. In recent years, however, spelling and punctuation have been highlighted as areas for improvement and this has led to course work and examinations allocating a mark to be added in for spelling. It could be a solution for you to mark spelling out of 1–3 at the end of an exercise. You don't necessarily have to do this each time, but include it regularly enough to demonstrate that you care. Notice too that in the case study above the teachers were instructed to correct spelling, and in the case study below how one of the teachers responds to a pupil's spelling difficulties. Don't ignore spelling but get it in proportion.

Responding to Pupils' Work

Your response to pupils' written work is a very important point of contact between you the the pupil and it plays a major part in shaping your relationship with the pupils. The case study below indicates how the pupils may feel about your response to their work.

CASE STUDY 7.3. FOR DISCUSSION/ACTION

As soon as we get our books back everyone looks immediately to see what mark they've got and says to each other, 'What did you get?' or 'I got so and so.' If you've got a low mark you try to lie low, but someone is bound to ask you, especially if he has done really well. If you get below a B, some teachers punish you by making you do it again in detention and Mr Briggs always makes a point of mentioning it in the next lesson, saying something like, 'Darren's mark was a notable exception to the high standard of the rest of the class....' Even if he says, 'Someone who shall be nameless let the rest of you down,' we always know who it is who got the lowest mark. What I hate most though are the teachers who get us to call out the marks to record in their mark books. Why don't they do it while they are marking? Sometimes I think it is just to humiliate the pupils they dislike most. (Darren, aged 13.)

For discussion:

How do the pupils in this class react to their teacher's marking – what is important for them?
What are the issues raised by this case study?

This case study highlights how seriously pupils take having their work marked, yet often it is a negative experience for them. This is largely because of their own emphasis on the marks they receive and how they stand in relation to other pupils, but they also dread the negative comments about their work made on the page or orally in class. In many cases pupils have come to view the teacher as judge, jury and hangman at the same time. A pupil who has written two or three sides and finds that the only comment you have written on his/her work is 'Spelling atrocious', is likely to feel deflated and wonder why s/he bothered. This does not mean that you have to be uncritical, as the pupils do need to know what they have done wrong and where they have made mistakes; rather it is a matter of how you do it. Criticism can be positive as well as negative, and it is important to show pupils how they can improve their performance next time. Always do your best to be seen to be fair and be able to justify what you have done. The most sensible approach is to follow the departmental guidelines where possible or the National Curriculum statements about levels or grades, and to list at the end of a piece of work what the pupil has achieved, eg: 'You have demonstrated that you can tell which idea is the most important and you have given some reasons.' The case study which follows illustrates the contrasting ways in which you can approach marking written assignments.

CASE STUDY 7.4. FOR ACTION/DISCUSSION

1. Examples of comments written by a teacher on a set of assignments:

Where are your corrections? See that they are done by next lesson!
This is not at all what I wanted. Try to follow the instructions!
This is very difficult to read. Try to be more legible and much tidier.
This is quite inadequate – do it again!
Finish it!

Compare the first set of comments with some written by a different teacher about a similar exercise:

Much better than last time.
There are still some mistakes but your written work is steadily improving. Keep it up!
Yes, you have got the point rather well. Now can you try to do something about your spelling as it rather lets you down.
Some good ideas here – what a pity you rather lost your way towards the end. Would it help if we planned the next essay together?
If you finish it, Michael, I'll mark it next time.
Well explained and well presented. Keep it up!
You have made some good points, Michael. Next time try to develop your ideas in more detail as this would help you score a higher mark.

What do these comments tell you? What do they indicate about the two teachers' approach to their task, their relationship with the group, expectations, etc? How are the pupils likely to react in each case?

2. Look at a set of books you have marked this term and see if a pattern emerges.

Are most of your comments about the work set or the pupils' spelling, legibility, etc.? What message does this convey?
Are the comments mainly positive or negative? What kind of advice are you giving?
How do you react to individual pupils? For example, if pupil X looked back on a series of your comments, how constructive would s/he find them?
How many of the books actually show pupils' work improving and how have you indicated this to the pupil?

How Do You Record Pupil Progress?

Keeping Your Mark Book

Your first essential is your mark book. Usually you will allot a page or so to each class or group that you teach. In your mark book you record the pupils' names, the numbers of any textbooks you may issue, the marks you award for each assignment and whether the pupil attended the lesson. Increasingly it is considered good practice to have a lesson register and often attendance is recorded in your mark book, though you may prefer to do this on your lesson record/plan. You may find that the school is using an optical mark reader to record pupil attainment for the National Curriculum. If this proves to be the case, someone will need to show you how to do this or input the results for you.

Whatever you do, make sure that your mark book is up-to-date because it is your first point of reference if you are asked about an individual pupil. Recording the marks in class by making the pupils call out their marks is one short cut, which will save you some time, but it is not popular with pupils because it highlights who did well and who did badly.

Reports

There is a legal requirement for the school to report pupils' progress regularly to parents and most schools have developed their own reports and Records of Achievement.

Feedback to pupils about their performance and progress is

very important. Case study 7.3 indicated just how much teacher feedback mattered to the pupils. Feedback can come orally through a teacher's comment to an individual pupil, or discussion with a pupil or group of pupils about how they are progressing. Most frequently, however, it is in writing through a report or pupil profile.

Some hints for successful report writing

- Take advice before you start. Each school has its own approach and house style – conform to it or you will become very unpopular. Ask your HOD or mentor what the procedure is and check whether there are any written guidelines.
- Allow plenty of time – it is very important to avoid errors, particularly on the type of report where all the subject teachers write on the same sheet. Writing reports will take much longer than you expect.
- If the report includes an element of negotiation with the pupils, allow even more time.
- Avoid nicknames, slang or grammatical errors. Reports are normally formal documents.
- Plan your comments before writing on the report form; this will help you avoid mistakes.
- Look at what other teachers have said. If your comments are vastly different from other people's, think about why this is so.
- Think about what you want to highlight about this particular pupil – effort, achievement, a particular skill, recent improvement, etc. The report form may have special slots for these items; if not, how are you going to get what you want to say into a rather small space?
- Give some thought to how you can make what you want to say intelligible to the pupils and their parents, especially as the language of reports tends to be rather bland.
- Find out whether you are allowed to take reports out of the staff room before you take them home.

CASE STUDY 7.5. FOR ACTION/DISCUSSION

This problem involves two NQTs:

Trevor has an enormous backlog of work. There are now seven assignments overdue and he appears extremely reluctant to do anything about it. Both attitude and effort leave much to be desired. (Report comment written by an NQT about a Year 10 pupil.)

Amal Ammitta, the form tutor of 10A, is summing up her form's reports and has noticed that Jennifer Trowson's reports comments are extremely negative. The example given above is perhaps the worst, but most of them are very critical of the pupils. Amal has only been teaching for two or three years herself, but the comments worry her because they stand out from all the others. Should she accept the comments as they stand, and if she does, how will the parents of her tutor group react? She knows from the year group progress meetings that several parents are likely to be unhappy about such strong criticism of their offspring. Moreover, if she does nothing, Jennifer will continue to write this kind of report. Would it be best to tackle Jennifer herself, or would it be wiser to act through the year head? Would speaking to Jennifer herself be less threatening and more productive than referring the problem upwards and, if so, how should she approach this difficult task? Would Jennifer perceive involving the year head as Amal getting her into trouble? How annoyed would the year head be if Amal acts without consulting him?

For action:

What advice would you give Amal in this difficult situation?

Jennifer, the subject teacher, has used the reports to put pressure on pupils. This highlights issues about her classroom management and relationships with the pupils. She is a conscientious teacher, anxious that her classes should do well, and she has piled on the work in order to encourage the pupils to practise their skills. They have proved resistant and the backlog of work has mounted up and is now becoming a trial of strength between teacher and pupils. Having failed to get cooperation, Jennifer is resorting to coercion, using the report to get the parents to put pressure on the pupils to do the work. As a strategy it is unlikely to improve her relationship with the pupils, but it is certainly gaining her the attention of other staff and it may result in her getting the help and advice she clearly needs. It also raises the question of why this situation has been allowed to go on for so long without attracting the attention of Jennifer's HOD. Jennifer clearly needs some training in report writing, particularly as nowadays there is usually an element of negotiation in the teacher's comments!

For action:
What advice would you give Jennifer?

Setting Homework

Why Do You Have to Set It?

If you have taught the pupils well, why do they need to do additional work at home? The fact that you regularly set your classes homework is not usually regarded as a sign of teacher failure. All too frequently how much homework a school sets is taken as a benchmark of its effectiveness. It gives out the message that learning is important to the institution and that it goes beyond school. Indeed parents often make judgements about a teacher based on the quantity and quality of the homework s/he sets. Homework should not, however, be merely a public relations exercise aimed at keeping parents happy and pupils occupied. What therefore are the educational objectives of setting homework?

- To provide additional practice in the skills currently being studied – reinforcement.
- To learn what they have been taught – revision.
- To enable individual research, eg, by looking up information in books provided by the school or by visiting libraries – inquiry/investigation.
- To prepare ahead – eg, translation.
- To plan an assignment – for discussion in the next session with the teacher.
- To do new work independently – opportunity for differentiated tasks.

This is quite a long list, yet it does not include the kind of homework task most frequently set by teachers. It is:

- To complete a task or piece of work for which there has been insufficient time during the lesson, ie finishing off work started in class.

If you find that you are doing this most of the time, do not worry; it does not mean that you are a bad teacher, rather it probably reflects the content-heavy nature of your subject and that you have to rely on homework in order to complete the syllabus. What you need to check is that there is variation in the tasks themselves and that from time to time you do set extension tasks. Try to avoid setting, 'Write up your notes for homework.'

Hints for Setting Homework

A clear and consistent approach to homework will secure you the best results, so establish the procedures that you are going to follow and stick to them.

Right at the beginning, check which days of the week have been allocated for homework for your groups, as this could affect how you teach and what homework you set. You could find, for example, that you teach one class on two successive days and that the homework comes between the two lessons. This could cause you problems and if you find out early enough, you may be able to renegotiate, otherwise you will have to plan around this factor.

Check how much time you have been allocated and try to keep to it. Sometimes it is difficult to set work of precisely the right length, but try to balance this out over two or three weeks.

Never take the pupils' word about when they should be doing homework. Ask the most appropriate person, eg, your mentor or HOD for the information that you need. Homework timetables are often produced by the year head, so s/he may be the best person to consult.

Some pupils will spend hours on their homework, others will spend next to no time on it. Try to get a feel of how individual pupils are coping with the work you set. Year 7 pupils are often very slow workers in the first term and you may need to take this into account when you set work.

Homework can provide an opportunity for challenging and differentiated tasks, but you need to approach this sensitively as it will highlight differences between pupils. It is also a time-consuming process.

If no logical homework exists, you don't have to invent some, but don't make a practice of not setting homework as the pupils will lose out and parents will begin to complain.

Remember that homework does not always have to be written.

Establish clear procedures for giving in homework — where, when. There should be no excuse for getting it wrong. Avoid accepting individual books on corridors as they tend to get lost.

Checking up and following up homework rigorously in the first few weeks will pay dividends later.

CASE STUDY 7.6. FOR ACTION

1. From the headteacher's post bag – some reactions to a new English teacher:

> Angela is having to spend all her time on her English homework this year and is working for up to six hours a night. We really feel that this is too much. Please could you arrange that the teacher concerned sets less time-consuming tasks. (Angela, Year 10.)

> I really must complain. Terry never seems to have any homework for English. I quiz him frequently and he tells me that none has been set or that he has finished all his work in school. (Terry, Year 9.)

> I really must object. The new English teacher set Miriam's class a piece of work which necessitated us going to the local library. I do not object to taking my daughter to the library, but I would prefer some notice. The homework had to be in the following morning and it was not at all convenient yesterday to take her to the nearest library which is some distance away. I should also like to point out that it took a considerable time to collect the information, then my daughter had to do a lengthy piece of written work to complete the assignment in order to meet the deadline. This seems to me quite unreasonable. (Miriam, Year 8.)

For action:

You are the NQT. What should you do in each of these cases?
You are the NQT's mentor. What advice should you give the NQT?

2. You are returning their exercise books to your Year 9 set. Arun's book is not there and you castigate him for not having given it in. 'I did give it in, Miss,' he says. The book isn't there and you have no recollection of it.

For action:

What actions should you take to deal with this situation?

CHAPTER 8

Being a Form Tutor

Coping with a Dual Role

CASE STUDY 8.1. FOR REFLECTION

When I went in on the day before the beginning of term, they told
me that I would be form tutor for 10K. At college they had said
that NQTs usually didn't have forms in their first year, but the
school said that there weren't enough full-time staff to do that,
especially since there were three NQTs this year, and anyway
they thought I would enjoy having a form!

Well, it certainly was another test for me as a teacher! There
was all the administrative stuff; it took me so long and the year
head always seemed to be going on at me because my returns
were late. There were 30 Year 10 pupils in my form. They were
nice kids, but they were very lively and boisterous, and it was hard
for me to establish a good relationship with pupils of that age and
they all seemed to need so much attention. It felt like having a
second job, and although I came to like my form a lot, and
actually did enjoy having them, I rather resented the amount of
time it took up when I could have been getting on with my lesson
preparation or marking. (NQT.)

As well as being a subject teacher, you are likely to be asked to
undertake responsibility for a form. The case study above
presents one NQT's reaction to becoming a form tutor and
highlights her ambivalent feelings about having to undertake a
dual role. It also indicates the difference between the new
teacher's expectations of what her duties were likely to be in the
first year and the school's perception of the situation.

Very few schools can afford the luxury of allowing a new

teacher not to have a form in the first year. Nor are you likely to be asked if you want one, or indeed given much choice of which form you get. The first time around you are likely simply to be allotted a form; most probably you will have to pick up the one that your predecessor in the post had last year. For many new teachers, this additional duty presents them with a very real challenge. It can be an onerous, difficult and time-consuming responsibility. It can also be extremely rewarding, but either way it involves a lot of hard work.

If you have to be a form tutor you will want to get it right and you will need to know what the job entails, so that you can cope with its demands. In the same way as with understanding your function as a subject teacher, it is sensible to start by consulting your job description as a form tutor, which will list all the tasks you have to carry out. A good job description will also help you clarify the main aspects of the role. The first point to notice is that the job description for a form tutor is as long as that for a subject teacher, yet it is a supplementary role. The NQI's comment in case study 8.1 that it felt like having a second job and that the two sets of duties make conflicting demands on her time is very pertinent.

An example of a form tutor's generic job description is given below as an exemplar and for reflection. Study it before you look at the analysis which follows the case study to see what it tells you about what this particular school expects of its form tutors. You may also want to compare it with the job description given to you by your own new school. If you have not been issued with a job description or list of duties as a form tutor, make sure that you ask your year head for one.

CASE STUDY 8.2. FOR REFLECTION

Bestwick Park High School – Form Tutor's Job Description

Most members of staff are asked to act as form tutors. The role of the form tutor is a responsible one and vital to the efficient running of the school and to successful pastoral care. For this aspect of the work, the form tutor is responsible to the head of year. The main functions are as follows:

1. Registration and Routine Business

The form tutor is responsible for the accurate daily marking of the form register (a vital legal document) and for seeing that all the information in the register is maintained up to date. Other returns of a routine nature should be dealt with as required, together with the distribution of information to parents. All absences must be accounted for by notes and any not so covered should be reported to the year head.

2. Reports and Records

The form tutor is responsible for the duplicate copies of reports. Any information of a confidential nature should be referred to the year head. The form tutor is expected to comment on reports and cover aspects of achievement and personality which are not covered by academic reports.

3. References and Special Reports

When appropriate, form tutors are expected to prepare, in consultation with colleagues, initial drafts for references, testimonials and special reports to outside agencies and the like.

4. Personal Appearance and Conduct

Form tutors are expected to monitor the personal appearance, eg, wearing of correct uniform, and behaviour of the members of their form and to insist on a reasonable standard.

5. Homework

In consultation with the head of year, form tutors should draw up a homework timetable for their form and, from time to time, check that it is adhered to satisfactorily by all pupils.

6. Form time

This time should be used purposefully and profitably in accordance with the programme of activities drawn up by the head of year and the member of staff with special responsibility for the personal, social and health education programme. THE FORM SHOULD REMAIN WITH THE FORM TUTOR IN THE ROOM ASSIGNED TO IT THROUGHOUT THIS PERIOD.

7. Assemblies

FORM TUTORS ARE EXPECTED TO ATTEND ASSEMBLIES WITH THEIR FORM AND TO SUPERVISE THE FORM'S MOVEMENT TO AND FROM THE FORM ROOM TO THE PLACE OF THE ASSEMBLY.

8. Year Meetings

Form tutors are expected to attend meetings as arranged in the school calendar and any others which might be necessary as called by the head of year.

9. Relations with Parents

It is hoped that parents would see form tutors at parents' meetings. Whenever possible form tutors will be involved when parents visit the school at other times. Form tutors should not arrange to see parents without reference to the head of year, who will consult senior staff before making any arrangements.

The form tutor should be the first person to whom a pupil will turn for help or advice, although it may be necessary to refer the matter to the year head, deputy head pastoral, head teacher or matron. Although some aspects of a form tutor's work may seem dull and routine, it is through regular daily contact that unobtrusive care is exercised.

Notes (same as subject teacher's job description).

The Bestwick Park form tutor's job description is a typical example of how a school views the role. It does not make easy reading, yet it does make it clear what the school expects of its tutors. The nine tasks set out in the job description describe:

■ when you are expected to be with your form, eg, at registration, in form time and at assembly. Being with your form during assembly and form time is highlighted by the use of capital letters. The school is stressing the importance of this task and hinting that there have been problems in the past
■ what your responsibilities are: eg, keeping registers accurately, seeing to the reports, distributing and collecting information, sorting out the form's homework timetable and monitoring uniform
■ what meetings you are expected to attend, eg, year meetings and parent's evenings.

There are, however, some things that it does not tell you. For example it does not tell you what to do in form time, except that it needs to be used purposefully and profitably and that you have to make sure that the pupils do not leave the form room and wander about the school.

Sometimes it is deliberately vague. For example, it mentions that you should follow the programme of activities drawn up by the year head or PSHE coordinator, which means that you will be teaching the form's PSHE, but it carefully avoids telling you that this means that you will be teaching the PSHE or what it will involve and this is a sensitive area about which you will need a lot of information. Similarly, it emphasizes that it is not prescribing how much time the various tasks will take and that it may not have listed everything, yet you will notice that it insists that your form tutor's duties are included in directed time, thus making them a compulsory part of your job. Thus there is a strong hint in the job description that there is more to being a form tutor than carrying out the tasks enumerated in this list.

What this job description does not show you very clearly is that in fact the form tutor's role covers three main areas of responsibility:

- for the routine administration of the form
- for the good conduct of the form
- for the pastoral care of the form.

In addition, the form tutor may have to teach PSHE to his/her form.

The functions listed at length in the Bestwick Park job description summarize most of the tasks connected with the first two aspects of the role and put most emphasis on the routine administration. Pastoral care is barely mentioned; it is implicit rather than explicit. Indeed the only mention is of 'unobtrusive care' and whereas this may reflect this particular school's priorities, it also indicates how the job actually works. A lot of your time will be spent on routine business, because this ensures the smooth and efficient running of the school, yet every now and then a pastoral issue will emerge, which will need sensitive handling.

In the sections that follow we shall discuss in turn each of the main areas of responsibility.

Managing the Routine Business

CASE STUDY 8.3. FOR ACTION

I hadn't realized that registers mattered so much. Most of the hassle I encountered in the first term was connected with my register. I hadn't got the names in before I met the form on the first morning of term and I never quite caught up. I failed to collect in all the necessary information. I couldn't remember what all those stupid signs meant and I kept getting them wrong. I didn't realize how crucial it was to have a reliable register monitor and didn't appoint one, so my register was never in the right place when matron wanted it, and she quickly decided that I was incompetent, especially as when she did find it, it was never complete. My year head was constantly irritated with me because matron kept grumbling about me to him, and finally when there was a dispute about a pupil's truancy and the evidence should have been in my register and it wasn't, because I still didn't know who they all were and who was there in the morning, the head herself, 'Had a little word'. I didn't enjoy that. I wish someone had explained about registers at the beginning. (NQT).

For discussion:

What are the lessons of this case study for a beginner teacher?

The case study highlights both the importance the school placed on the correct keeping of registers and the trouble that this new teacher built up for himself when he failed to carry out this task efficiently. Getting your register right gets you off to a good start. The school was not just being fussy, registers *do* matter:

- Registers are legal documents – accuracy does matter as you can be dismissed for falsifying a register.
- Registers get used, for example by education welfare officers checking for truancy, so the information does need to be accurate and readily available. If your register isn't where it should be and up-to-date, your year head and other senior staff will become irritated because it will cause them difficulties and they are going to think that you are inefficient and begin to doubt your competence.
- If you allow pupils to take the register for you, or take their word about things that you should check out for yourself, you are inviting trouble. Wrong information about who was present at the time can easily be recorded and the form will know that they can take advantage of you. Whatever your class tell you, remember that pupils are not allowed to fill in the register: it has to be done by a member of staff.

The new teacher in the case study above might have found life easier if he had read and followed the instructions.

Because of the number of symbols involved and the need to get it right, most schools provide some form of briefing sheet or guidance on how to complete the register The most obvious place to look is in the staff handbook, or in the register itself. If you can't locate it, ask the year head or your mentor where it is, or seek advice before you fill in any information about your form. An exemplar from Bestwick Park High School will show you the kind of information you should expect to be available.

CASE STUDY 8.4. EXEMPLAR: GUIDELINES FOR KEEPING A REGISTER

Bestwick Park High School – Records Of Attendance

These are the responsibility of form teachers and should be available for inspection at any time and be as complete as possible. Addresses and telephone numbers should be kept up-to-date and amendments sent to the office as soon as they are received.

Registers should be marked at the beginning of each morning and afternoon session. Every pupil on the register must be marked / (present) or O (absent). The pupil must not be marked as present if s/he is not in the room.

Any pupil marked absent who is subsequently found to have made an attendance should have a suitable letter inserted in the absence section in accordance with the instructions in the front of the register. A list is given below:

Symbols for registers
Present: / diagonal strokes in blue or black.
Authorized absence:

Coach late	C
Discretionary authorized absence	D
Educational visit/trip	V
Holiday	H
Illness	M
Interview	I
Late	L

How can a briefing sheet help you?

■ It clarifies what information you need to record in your register.
■ It tells you clearly when to mark the register.
■ It tells you what to do about various types of absence and provides you with a list of symbols to use.

Some Hints for Dealing with Registers

■ Read the briefing sheet carefully and make sure you follow the instructions.
■ Start the term with your register ready (use pencil initially if in doubt).
■ Consult about anything that is not clear to you. Your year

head is your first port of call. If s/he seems too busy or uninterested in your problem, go and see the person with responsibility for NQTs and get him/her to go through with you what is required.

■ Make sure that you have an up-to-date list of the symbols – they keep changing! Keep it to hand and refer to it constantly. This is one area where it is not a good idea to put your trust in your unaided memory. If the school uses a mechanical or computer system for clocking pupils in, get someone to show you how it operates and what you have to do.

■ Never let a pupil mark the register!

■ Refer any dubious absences to your year head. Delay in passing on information could mean trouble for you later.

Responsibility for the Good Conduct of the Form

CASE STUDY 8.5. FOR ACTION

I couldn't be bothered with the trivia....

The school seemed to put a great deal of emphasis on things that seemed to me to be very trivial indeed. At first I did my best with the never ending list of administrative tasks that the year head kept unloading onto me: organizing the homework timetable, collecting school fund, carrying out uniform checks and distributing the endless letters home about this or that. I felt like some kind of postman. I was always giving out letters and collecting in reply slips and most of it seemed singularly unimportant. This wasn't why I became a teacher. I got very fed up with all the administration and after a while I didn't bother all that much. I seemed to be getting on with my form very well, and after all that was what really mattered, and they seemed to share my attitude to what I had come to feel was the school's mania for bureaucracy.

Then in my second term, my year head suddenly turned on me. He said that I was completely letting myself go. I couldn't understand what the problem was, as I thought everything was fine, so he kindly explained what he meant. Everything was in a mess, he said. None of the paperwork was done, and what was worse, the form's attitude was slipping. 'I hope,' he said, 'that this isn't a reflection of your own attitude.' I tried to put my point of view about things, but that only seemed to incense him. He really wasn't open-minded on the issue. In fact he said categorically that in his opinion I was failing in my duties as a form tutor and was allowing my form to get completely out of hand. It was affecting their attitude to other staff, he said, and to school activities. It was already noticeable that none of my form were volunteering for anything, and in this school Year 7 pupils always volunteer for everything. A lot of them were already regularly in detention for other subject staff, yet it was only their second term in the school. Something was going very wrong with my form, and he held me at least partly responsible. If I didn't pull up my socks, he said, he would have to refer the whole matter to the deputy head with responsibility for the pastoral system and it could affect whether I passed my first year. (Form tutor.)

For action:

What advice would you give this form tutor and on what grounds?
Who do you think is the most at fault in this conflict – the tutor or the year head?
How would you rectify this situation?

CASE STUDY 8.6. FOR ACTION

I always meant to be early. . . .

The year head kept popping into my form room at registration time with things she wanted to give me or to see a pupil. Sometimes she was there before I had arrived and that was embarrassing. I did mean to be early, but there were so many other things that I had to do in the mornings connected with my subject responsibility, and in the afternoons there was so little time. In fact the teachers coming in to use my room for the first lesson in the afternoon seemed to be rather irritated with me, and I began to sense that they felt that my registration was taking too long. Then my head of department said that there had been some complaints about the state of my room from other subject staff because of all the stuff that I had on the desk and the children's stuff cluttering up the room, and the senior staff began to murmur about the litter left by my form after lunch. Such a lot of fuss about a little mess. Then came the morning that the whole senior assembly had to wait because my form was very late because I just didn't notice the time and now the year head has said that it is time that we had a talk about how I organize form affairs. (Form tutor.)

For action:

What advice would you give this form tutor and on what grounds?
What help should s/he be receiving from the year head?
In what ways might the form tutor's organizational difficulties affect the form?
How would you rectify the situation?

CASE STUDY 8.7. FOR ACTION

He's never there

Chris simply doesn't seem to have taken on board his form responsibilities. His head of department speaks highly of his commitment and his good ideas, but I can't say the same about him as a form tutor. Whenever I have to visit his form at registration or form time, he's missing, at any rate he's not in the room with the pupils. I let it go a few times and then I spoke to him about it. He said, 'OK' and that he wouldn't do it again. He said that it was an emergency and that he'd had to attend to something, but the next time I went on my rounds, he was out of the room again and when I eventually found him, he was busy sorting out some equipment that he wanted to use later that morning for his teaching.

Form time is the one decent patch of time a tutor gets with his form. It's not intended to be an extra preparation or marking period and anyway you can't just leave the pupils on their own in a classroom like that. (Year head grumbling about a tutor.)

For action:
What advice would you give this tutor and on what grounds?
What effect is this tutor's behaviour likely to have on the conduct of this form?
What approach should the year head adopt in order to rectify the situation?

CASE STUDY 8.8 FOR ACTION

She was sitting on his desk!

It's not just that the form is becoming very rowdy; when I went into the form room this morning, there was Mary-Anne sitting on his desk, chatting away to him and it wasn't the first time either. He just doesn't seem to know how to keep them at a distance or to have any idea about what is appropriate behaviour for a good looking young teacher with a Year 11 form. Dressed in jeans like that, he looks like one of the Sixth Form and I'm not surprised that they take advantage of him. I've heard a rumour that he's invited some of them home, but I don't know whether it's true or not.

After I saw him with Mary-Anne again at lunchtime, I thought I must do something, so I had a word with him, but he just laughed and said that she was talking to him about some home problems, and that he thought it was part of his job to sort out his form's pastoral problems. He doesn't seem to realize what kind of effect he is having. I knew it was a mistake to give him a Year 11 form. It wouldn't have been anything like so bad a problem if he had been given a Year 7 group. (Worried year head talking to a colleague.)

For action:

What advice would you give this form tutor and on what grounds?
What are the issues involved in the case study?
What approach should the year head adopt?
How can the situation be rectified?

These case studies highlight a number of important aspects of your role as a form tutor.

First they highlight the number of routine tasks that you have to carry out as a form tutor. Many of them are in themselves humdrum, trivial, time-consuming and dreary, but they keep the school going. Avoiding them or failing to carry them out affects a lot of other people and will in the end only cause trouble for you and make you thoroughly unpopular with your colleagues.

Second, while illustrating how important it is to be on top of the routine demands, they highlight the close link between those routine procedures and good conduct. Once you have arrived late for registration, you set up a cycle of things that you don't quite manage to achieve that day – or the next, and pretty soon your form is the one that is always late, and you, and the form, acquire a reputation. The whole way you conduct the affairs of your form – your organizational effectiveness as a tutor, good timekeeping, keeping your room tidy and uncluttered, seeing that your form is in uniform, seeing that it gets to assembly on time and doesn't keep other people waiting – is an important aspect of good teaching because it enables the teaching and learning to take place and because it helps to maintain a good standard of behaviour on the part of the pupils.

Third, they highlight the conflict that is likely to occur between your two roles, subject teacher and form tutor, as both begin to make demands upon your time. In teaching, time management is often a problem, not just for new teachers, and this is an issue that we shall discuss more fully in Chapter 10. Here we shall simply point out that if you concentrate on one role at the expense of the other you will create a new set of problems for yourself. The tutor who spent form time preparing his equipment failed to carry out his duty of care for his form as he was responsible for their safety and good conduct at the time. However, he wasn't just negligent in leaving them: the pupils will have got the impression that he didn't care what they did or how they behaved during form time.

Fourth, they highlight how careful you have to be to develop the right sort of good relationship with your form. The pupils will be very quick to pick up and, if it suits them, adopt your attitudes. If you are late, they will be late because they know that they can get away with it as you won't be there anyway. If you can't be bothered to check their uniform, they won't bother to wear it. If you don't notice their jewellery, they will wear it. They will react swiftly to your standard and your actions or inaction will provide them with an unspoken message about what to expect. Most importantly, if you seem at all critical of the system, they begin to mirror your views, and this could affect the behaviour of the class adversely.

The degree of formality you will need to adopt with your form will of course vary with the group concerned and the type and ethos of school, but particularly at first you would be well advised to be more formal rather than less. It is important to establish a distance between yourself and the pupils nearest to you in age, and particularly important not to become inadvertently the central figure in the latest piece of school gossip.

CASE STUDY 8.9. FOR ACTION

It's the third time I've caught Billy Rose skiving off assembly. I've put him in detention for Monday evening, but it's really Fred, his tutor, I'd like to put into detention. If he accompanied his form to assembly, Billy wouldn't be able to dodge off like that. When I mentioned to Fred that I'd caught Billy, he looked surprised and said that they were all there as far as he knew when they left the form room, but he had needed to collect something from the staff room, so he hadn't gone downstairs with them. I was cross enough to point out that it wasn't the first time it had happened and eventually he said that he'd keep an eye on Billy. I suspect that even if he set out with the whole class, Fred would not know how many he still had on arrival, and that others besides Billy are skipping off on the way. Billy is simply not very good at getting away with it. Are all NQTs as wet as this I wonder? (Duty team leader grumbling to a colleague about an NQT.)

For action:

What advice would you give Fred and on what grounds?
What are the issues raised by this case study?
How would you resolve the situation?

CASE STUDY 8.10. FOR ACTION

'Please Sir, it wasn't me. I didn't do it.' Jimmy has come to the staff room door to tell you, as his form tutor, that he is innocent. Innocent of what, you will wonder, as you don't have a clue why he feels he has to protest his innocence or what he is supposed to have done.

For action:

Sometimes you have to be a detective – how do you set about dealing with this problem?
Clearly Jimmy sees you as a source of help – what is your role as Jimmy's form tutor?

Responsibility for Pastoral Care

The job description featured earlier in the chapter gives you very little guidance about how to carry out your pastoral responsibility for your form and you may well be wondering what precisely is expected of you and what your role entails.

This part of your job is about your responsibility for the welfare of the members of your form. What kind of problem or issue is a responsibility of this nature likely to involve?

An example: Terry is persistently late all this term – is there more to it than a punctuality problem? When you investigate you find that Terry's punctuality problem is caused by a home problem: his journey to school is difficult and his Mother usually brings him in the car. Recently she has been ill, so he is coming on two buses and the times don't fit. His teachers need to be told that there is a problem and that it could last for the rest of term.

Terry's problem is relatively straightforward; others with which you will have to deal might be more complex; for instance:

Several teachers have mentioned that Donovan's work has deteriorated lately.

Jenny is looking rather listless — her friends come to you because they are worried about her.

You notice that Deborah always seems to be hanging about with two girls from Year 11 — does it mean anything?

Anil says that some Year 10 boys have been picking on him at lunchtime and at the bus stop.

These examples illustrate the kind of problem with which you may have to deal. You can't tell whether they are really serious until you start to investigate. Donovan's work could be deteriorating for all kinds of reasons — home, school or both. He may have a pastoral problem or he may simply be finding the work difficult and need some help; either way you have to look into the problem. Does it really matter that Deborah's friends seem to be girls two years older than her? Again you have to try to find out why this is happening. Deborah may be seeking friends among the more senior girls because she has fallen out with her friends in her year group, or more likely because problems at home have caused her to seek to replace the relationships that are not working at home, with one involving older girls at school. Anil's complaint may reveal both a bullying and a racism problem which will need attention. It is your job to find out as far as you can what is causing a pupil to act in a way that is drawing attention to his/her behaviour.

How demanding it will prove to be will vary. Some form tutors find that they have a relatively easy passage, others that a whole cluster of problems occur at the same time — the demands of pastoral care are unpredictable. It is unlikely that as a beginner teacher you will have deliberately been given a particularly difficult form, but there easily could be one or two pupils who, for one reason or another, are causing concern.

How do you know that a pupil is 'causing concern'? The examples above give some indication of how you are likely to find out about pastoral problems in your form. Sometimes a pupil will come to you for advice or, like Anil, because they want to tell you something is wrong. Sometimes other pupils will come to you and say, for example, 'We are worried about Jenny.' Sometimes other teachers will draw your attention to it, and their comments may tell you something you haven't realized about a particular pupil, for example, 'Jenny is looking rather listless, don't you think? Is it because her father is working abroad again?' Usually however, you will realize that there is a problem because in some way or another the pupil will be acting in such a way that will eventually attract attention to his/her behaviour.

Once you are aware that a problem exists, what is your role in dealing with it? How far are you as the form tutor expected to solve the problem personally? The two case studies which follow are intended to help you explore what your role as form tutor should be.

CASE STUDY 8.11. FOR ACTION

She doesn't seem to have any friends.

By the time I had had the form for about half a term, I began to notice that Usma Samani was always alone. I asked a few of the form about her and they said that she had come new to the school towards the end of last year and that although they had tried to be friendly, she did not want to mix in, so after a while they had given up. Later on when I spoke to one of the nicest girls on her own, Tracy said that some of the form had been really nasty to Usma, moving her things from where she had put them, and generally being rather rough. There was no actual name-calling, Tracy said, when I probed a bit further, nothing overtly racist, but they definitely hadn't made her welcome and as a result, Usma kept out of their way. I tried to talk to Usma about it, but she says that there is nothing wrong, so what should I do next? (NQT.)

For action:

What should this new teacher do about Usma Samani?
What are the issues raised in this case study?
Where can the tutor expect to find help?
What should the tutor's role be in dealing with a problem of this nature?
Compare this problem with case study 5.7 in Chapter 5. What are the similarities?

CASE STUDY 8.12. FOR ACTION

They said I was over-involved.

I can't see what else I was supposed to do. Ruth's friends came to me and said that she was so unhappy that she might commit suicide. They said that they knew that she was cutting her arm with a knife. Naturally I was very concerned. I talked to Ruth and it did seem to help her. I think she really wanted someone to talk to. She told me that her mother had left home a couple of years ago and gone off with someone else. Her parents were divorced now. It had been alright at first but now her father had a serious girlfriend, Liz, and Ruth thought Liz was awful. She showed me her arm without my having to ask her, and there were nasty cuts all the way up. It looked dreadful and I was really frightened that she would do something worse next time.

I had to tell the year head, although it seemed like breaking a confidence. Her friends and I were so worried about Ruth that I felt that I had no choice, but this actually made things more difficult: Ruth liked talking to me and confided in me a lot, but the year head was adamant that I should keep a low profile with Ruth. The year head said that what Ruth wanted was attention and that talking to her about her problems encouraged her to act destructively.

I did try to follow the year head's instruction to discourage Ruth, but she kept coming up to me at every opportunity – form time, in the lunch hour and even after school. I didn't like to send her away. She was so unhappy and I was afraid about what would happen if I rejected her. The year head said she had referred it to the deputy head and that I should leave it to her to sort out, but nobody seemed to be doing anything positive to help Ruth, and in the meantime it got worse, so how could I send her away?

Then the deputy head came to see me and was really annoyed with me. She said that they had it all in hand, and that she had seen Ruth's father who was referring her to the Child Guidance Clinic to see a psychologist and that I was not to interfere. She said that I was becoming over-involved. (NQT talking to a friend.)

For action:

What advice would you give this teacher and on what grounds?
What are the issues raised by this case study?
What kind of a role should a form tutor play in a case of this sensitivity?

Some Guidelines in Dealing with Pastoral Problems

Be aware — your first responsibility is to notice the problem. If, like Chris, in case study 8.7, you are so preoccupied with your subject teaching that you are neglectful of your form, you will not notice problems and they will build up.

Once you have become aware that there seems to be a problem, the next step is to do some investigation, so that you can find out how serious the problem really is. In the example at the beginning of this section, the tutor asked Terry about his recent and persistent lateness, and it quickly became clear that it was essentially a transport problem, but one connected with his mother's illness which could also have an effect on Terry's progress.

It is most unwise to keep a problem totally to yourself as it could easily lead to trouble later. It is your duty to put your year or house head, who is your line manager in pastoral matters, in the picture as soon as you become clear that there is a problem.

Confidentiality is a problem, but the advice here is never to promise confidentiality as you cannot always keep to it, and there are some issues, eg drugs, where it simply doesn't apply.

If you are reasonably sure that you want to deal with the problem yourself, make this quite clear to the year head, and explain what steps you are proposing to take. Most probably the year head will be pleased that you are not simply unloading a matter which you can easily resolve yourself and that you are showing some initiative.

If you are in doubt or it is a sensitive issue, then referring the problem upwards is the natural solution for you. Discussing the matter with your year head enables you to explore all the possible strategies and make an assessment of the situation.

Clarify your role in what happens next. It is important that all the people who become involved are clear about their various roles, otherwise a pupil can easily play one teacher off against another and begin to manipulate the situation.

If the year head or one of the senior management team becomes involved and takes over, do try to follow the instructions, as you may unwittingly make a delicate situation more difficult. If it doesn't make sense to you, or it seems a risky strategy, ask for an explanation. If you don't understand or disagree with the official line, talk to your mentor. In the case study about Ruth, the tutor didn't really understand why she shouldn't talk to Ruth, when it was what the girl wanted and it seemed to help. Because she had no previous experience of this kind of problem, the tutor didn't recognize or understand signs such as the pupil's eagerness to show off the cuts to friends and to the tutor, which indicated to more experienced staff Ruth's need for attention and professional help. Similarly she found it difficult to believe that she was encouraging a pupil's acts of self destruction, rather than helping a girl in need. So if in doubt, always talk it through as it will help you understand aspects of a case which might not otherwise make sense to you.

You have the right to be kept informed of what steps are being taken. Indeed if you are kept in total ignorance, you may make some mistakes which could adversely affect the situation and which could have been avoided. Sometimes things happen so rapidly that it is difficult to keep everyone up-to-date. At other times it can take a while for important information to be disseminated, but if weeks go by and no one tells you what is happening, go and ask the year head for information. In the case study about Ruth, it would have reassured the tutor to know that the deputy had seen Ruth's father and that professional help was being sought, and allayed her concern that nothing was being done about the case.

Be patient, as, especially when outside agencies are involved, the process takes a while. If nothing seems to be happening, by all means check up that it hasn't been forgotten, but consult rather than act unilaterally. If you intervene without consulting the others involved, the effect could be disastrous and you could be blamed.

CASE STUDY 8.13. FOR ACTION/DISCUSSION

There is a suspicious bruise on Darren's neck when he arrives late for registration one morning.

For action/discussion:

What do you do?
What are your responsibilities as Darren's form tutor?

CASE STUDY 8.14. FOR ACTION/DISCUSSION

Christine didn't answer to her name when I called the register, so I repeated it and she burst into tears. Andrea said that Christine's mother had left home at the weekend. (NQT.)

For action/ discussion:

As Christine's form tutor how should you deal with this situation?

CHAPTER 9

Dealing with Parents

'Parents are always welcome', says the school prospectus. Meeting parents has become a vital part of the school's public relations. In what capacity will you as an NQT have to deal with parents and how should you go about it? You will meet parents mainly in two capacities:

- as a subject teacher
- as the form tutor of their child.

You are likely to have contact with parents:

- at parents' meetings to discuss progress
- through letters/communications expressing concern about some aspect of their child's progress
- when they make a scheduled/unscheduled visit to the school
- when they assist teachers in the classroom, school library or help with expeditions
- at school functions.

You may feel apprehensive about how you will manage these contacts. Younger teachers often feel at a disadvantage with parents because their lack of experience, seniority and confidence are all too apparent to the parents. At 22 or 23 you may well seem to parents hardly more mature than the pupils for whose progress you are responsible and they are more likely to challenge you than they would somebody older, even if s/he is also a new entrant to the profession.

Dealing with your First Parents' Meeting

Your first parents' meeting is likely to occur when you have only been in the school for a few weeks. If you make a poor impression at this time, it could lead to a group of parents questioning your competence as a teacher. This kind of thing escalates and you could find yourself with the kind of reputation you would prefer to avoid. The case study below gives an extreme example of what could happen.

CASE STUDY 9.1. FOR ACTION/DISCUSSION

Urgent memo from the headteacher to the head of department:

> I had a whole stream of parents last night at the Year 10 parents' meeting, coming to complain about Miss X. She seems to have been extremely aggressive, complaining about the performance or the behaviour of child after child. She really set the backs up of those parents, and each in turn complained about her manner as well as her teaching. They claimed that she was not marking the work, homework was not being set, or at least their child never seemed to have any, and that she was not covering the syllabus, and they compared her adversely with Mrs Y, who is teaching the parallel group. Each set of parents said that it was not that they considered their child to be a little angel, but that on the whole s/he was performing satisfactorily in other subjects, and that they felt Miss X was over-critical, indeed several said that they felt that she was picking on their child. They were all very concerned about their child's progress, but each set of parents felt that the problem was with the teacher, not their child!
>
> I said that we would look into the situation and come back to them. Please will you, as the head of department concerned, investigate the matter and come to see me to discuss the problem asap. We shall need to think about what strategies we must apply to retrieve the situation.

For action/discussion:

What mistakes had this NQT made in handling the parents' meeting?
How can you be confident and assertive with parents without being considered aggressive?
How can the situation be retrieved? Prepare an action plan for 1) the HOD and 2) the NQT.

The case study above illustrates how important it is to handle that first parents' evening successfully, so how do you go about it?

The first thing to remember is that you may be nervous about meeting the parents, but many of them will be apprehensive about meeting the teachers and about how well or badly their child is progressing. This gives you a weapon, but be careful about how you use it. The case study above demonstrates just what can happen if you attack too much or too forcefully.

Lest you get the wrong impression from the case study, which made its point by giving an example of poor practice, we should say that most meetings with parents go well. Both sides have the pupil's interests at heart and know that they will be achieved best by cooperation and good will. Only a very small number of parents at any meeting will make difficulties, but the problem is that even one set of difficult parents can colour the whole evening for you, and you want if possible to avoid this kind of experience. Whatever you do, there will be the occasional very difficult person to deal with, but if you prepare for the meeting, you can eliminate the avoidable disasters. There are a number of ways in which you can do this, outlined below.

If, for example, you are teaching a sixth form group together with another teacher, you could arrange to operate as a pair, seeing the parents together. This can make the occasion much less threatening for you. You may also find it useful the first time to run through your comments with your HOD or mentor and take advice on the best way to express your opinions.

Your appearance and your manner can help you. Beware of dressing too casually or looking too young. You need to look like a professional – personifying for the group of parents, their image of a teacher. This is an occasion when wearing a suit might help you; so might a touch of formality, such as standing up to shake hands with each set of parents as you begin or end the interview. It gives you control of the proceedings and looks professional.

Knowing the names of your teaching group is a great confidence-booster. You will probably notice in the staffroom in the week before a Year 7 meeting, especially if it is in the Autumn term, a lot of teachers spending time gazing at the pupils' record photos. This is because all the pupils in Year 7 are new to the staff and they are trying to fix the faces in their memory to ensure that they talk about the right pupil. You are in this position for all your classes, and could adopt this approach with other year groups besides Year 7, especially where you teach the pupils in form units. It will take quite a time to find the pictures if the pupils are taught in sets. Another strategy that is acceptable for Year 7, as the parents will understand that all the year group are new, is to photocopy the set of record photos for the form that you teach, and have them with you at the parents' meeting. What you want to avoid saying is, 'Who's she?' or, 'Do I teach him?' Neither of these questions will reassure an anxious parent. Experienced teachers usually spend a little time in the lessons in the run up to a parents' meeting checking that they can identify the pupils. 'This is the class with four Elizabeths. I know that you are called Elizabeth, just remind me of your surname, so that I do not confuse you with the others.'

Make sure that your marking is up-to-date. This will pre-empt personal criticism as well as providing you with a better basis for discussion. Check your mark book to see what profile emerges for each child, as this is your record of what has been achieved. Be careful about letting the pupils see the mark book, as they could seize on things or make unfortunate comparisons with other pupils in the group. You may find it useful to have a piece of work or the pupil's exercise book with you at the meeting; this is often helpful when you are trying to explain to a parent precisely what is the difficulty that the pupil is experiencing.

Check what you have written in the pupil's exercise book recently or, for a parents' meeting which takes place in the Spring or Summer terms, check what you wrote on the pupil's report. This could prevent you from contradicting yourself at the meeting, or you could comment on progress since the report.

Be guarded about predictions, especially for public examinations or UCAS. Check the school policy about predictions and explain this to parents if necessary, and tell them that all kinds of factors could influence performance in the months ahead.

Keep to time, especially if there is an appointments system. Parents get very irritated if they have to wait for ages or you are running very much behind time. Monitor yourself during the first meeting to check whether you have a problem in this respect. You may find that you need to bring an interview to an end by referring to the time and the number of parents waiting.

Be constructive even when you can't be positive. Sound as if you like the child, listen to what the parents say, and don't, whatever you do, compare him/her with some other child in the group as this almost always has repercussions. Try to have some suggestions to offer, 'We can try this approach . . .' so that you do not suggest that the situation or the child is quite hopeless!

Be analytical — this also emphasizes that you are being professional and not personal in your criticism of their child. Again your analysis of what is going wrong will lead you on to discuss possible approaches and solutions. It is important that the parent realizes that you are working with the pupil in order to help him/her improve and not simply writing off their child as no good at your subject.

Try to create a partnership rather than allowing a 'them and us' situation to develop. For example using 'We' rather than 'I' helps to create a feeling that you are working together. Sometimes a parent will ask, 'What can we do to help our child?' Don't reject this kind of overture even if it is difficult to think of how the parents can assist. Offer to keep them fully informed of how the situation develops so that they will at least know what progress is being made.

What Do You Do if the Pupil is Experiencing Problems?

Don't fudge the issue, ie don't pretend that the pupil is OK when s/he is about to have a real disaster. Problems don't go away if you ignore them; usually they get worse, and the last thing that you want is to have to explain to the headteacher when the inevitable complaint comes, 'Why weren't we told that there was a problem?' Similarly avoid, 'Yes, I know she's hopeless at this subject, but she's a very reliable book monitor', this sounds like you have given up and are fobbing the parents off with soft soap.

Being analytical is probably the best approach, as it depersonalizes the problem, which makes it more acceptable for the parents. Taking this kind of approach could make them more inclined to trust your judgement as to how serious the problem is because it shows that you have recognized that a problem exists and have assessed what it is about. Give them some hope by suggesting what the pupil can do in order to improve.

Sometimes there is a real gap in perception between the parents and the teacher. Sometimes the parents are over-ambitious and pushing their child too hard. Sometimes the pupil has desperately pretended that things are not as bad as they turn out to be. Some parents will remain convinced that they have produced a genius whatever you do or say. Handle this kind of situation as constructively as you can. Don't be afraid to bring a second opinion, eg your HOD, or a member of the senior management team. Try not to let it develop into an unpleasant incident, and if they are too difficult or time-consuming, you will have to say, 'This in my judgement is what the situation is; if we cannot agree, I shall have to refer you to ...' If you think a particular pupil's progress might cause this kind of problem, consult your HOD before the meeting so that you are both prepared.

Communicating with Parents

CASE STUDY 9.2. FOR ACTION

Catriona Scott's postbag

Some time after the parents' meeting for her Year 7 tutor group, Catriona Scott received these communications from parents of her tutor group. You are Catriona Scott, NQT form tutor to 7S. How would you deal with each of the following:

1. Dear Miss Scott,

We were unable to attend the recent parents' evening, but would like to meet Bobby's teachers to discuss his progress. Please will you arrange this for us. A Wednesday afternoon would be most convenient for us.

Yours sincerely,

Jennifer Phelps, Mrs (parent of Robert, 7S)

2. Dear Miss Scott,

At the parents' meeting you said that Erica seemed to be rather isolated within the form. At the time we hoped that as term progressed, she would settle in better, or that you would take the necessary steps to deal with the problem. We are therefore disappointed to see that far from any improvement, the situation seems to have worsened. Erica came home yesterday very distressed because there were two lessons, games and English, in which she was left without a partner. We hope that the matter will be expedited, and that Erica will experience no further problems of this sort.

Yours sincerely,

Arthur Brown (daughter – Erica Brown, 7S)

It is your clear recollection that at the parents' meeting Mr and Mrs Brown had insisted that no problem existed.

3. Dear Miss Scott,

When I told you at the parents' meeting that Gary never seems to have any homework, you said that you would check that he was receiving sufficient. He still seems to have no homework to do in the evenings, and when I ask him about this, either he says that he did it all at lunch time or that none was set. Please could I have some definite information about what homework is being set for Gary's form?

Yours faithfully,

Sharon Davies (mother of Gary, 7S)

You asked some of Gary's teachers, but they laughed and said that this kind of thing was an old chestnut: parents were always claiming that homework wasn't being set, when what they meant was that, like a lot of boys of that age, however much work had really been set, Gary was just dashing off his homework in a few minutes.

4. Dear Miss Scott,

I heard from a friend that there has recently been a parents' meeting for Gary's year group. When Gary joined the school in September, I asked to be informed of such events separately from Gary's mother as we are in the process of divorcing. Now I find that I have missed a meeting which would have given me information about my son's progress. Can you please ensure that in future I am informed about all school functions which I should attend, and could you let me know when it would be convenient for me to come to see you to discuss Gary's progress?

Yours sincerely,

Evan Davies (father of Gary, 7S)

You do not know what arrangements have been made and are unsure what the procedures are for supplying information to divorcing fathers.

From time to time you will receive letters or 'phone calls from parents. The majority of these will be from the parents of the pupils in your form or tutor group, as the parents are likely to see you as the first point of contact to express their concerns about their child.

Although the letters in Miss Scott's postbag have been geared to a Year 7 parents' evening, they are not untypical of the kind of communication you could receive. The first piece of advice about such communications is that, unless they are purely routine, never attempt to deal with them on your own: share them with a colleague. Usually a sensible starting point is to take the letter to the head of year and seek advice. Don't feel slighted if the reply is drafted by someone more senior than you: it is in order to protect you.

All the letters involve other colleagues as well as you. Letters 1 and 3 will be unpopular with colleagues because both make demands on them. When they have just spent a tiring evening seeing a succession of parents, they are rarely keen to make additional appointments to see parents, who, for one reason or another, couldn't make it, yet of course, as part of the public relations process, appointments will have to be arranged. This kind of thing is normally done by the head of year, usually in consultation with one of the deputies. Some schools follow the policy of arranging a session for the parents with the form tutor, or head of year, who will report to parents what the other teachers have said, so you will need to check what the normal procedure is. If real difficulties emerge, or if the appointments can't be fixed with all the teachers concerned, a written report is sometimes completed and sent home.

Checking up on other teachers always irritates them. the homework issue is indeed an old and perennial chestnut. There is very rarely no homework set. More often the problem lies in one subject and sometimes in the parents' understanding of the tasks set. As an NQT you may find it embarrassing to handle, because experienced teachers may resent an NQT checking up on them. Talk it through with the head of year, who is likely to know the state of play about homework. Is anyone else making the same complaint? You will obviously have to check Gary's homework to see how much he is doing. A common procedure in many schools is to use a homework diary, which parents see daily and have to sign daily or weekly, and this service could be offered to Gary's mother. She may of course be over-anxious because of the family circumstances indicated in letter 4, but using a homework diary should monitor the problem effectively. You will have to check it weekly, which is extra work for you, but it should pay dividends.

Letter 4 raises the issue of how to treat parents who are divorced or separated. Miss Scott has not been told about an arrangement for Gary's father to receive communications, and this puts her in a difficult position. Before a parents' meeting you should check whether any pupil will be represented by more than one set of parents/guardians and precisely what arrangements have been made. The other staff teaching the pupils concerned will also need to be informed, so that they don't make insensitive remarks, or fail to wait for the second set of parents. Some pupils will need two sets of reports sent home. If you receive a letter like letter 4, however, do check before you do anything else that it really has been agreed that the father should receive this information, otherwise you may find yourself being used as a pawn in a difficult divorce.

At least two of the letters referred to something you had said at the parents' meeting, or promised to do after it. If you say that you will investigate something for a parent, you must report back. Even if you find that nothing is wrong, it is only courteous to reassure the parents. Similarly, letters need a prompt reply, even if only to say, 'We are dealing with the matter and will come back to you as soon as possible.'

If the letter says, 'You said ...' it tends to sound aggressive, as if the parents are on the attack, and you need to be very careful about how you deal with it. When you receive a letter which appears critical, demanding or unjust, avoid the temptation to write back in the same style. Any letter should be courteous and responsive. If your recollection of the discussion is altogether different from the parents', it could be difficult and probably unproductive to try and prove this. Letter 2 raises a difficult problem about how a pupil is integrating into the form, and this should not be side-tracked into an argument about what you said at the meeting. Whether or not these parents acknowledged the existence of a problem when they saw you at the parents' meeting, now they clearly accept that a serious problem exists. This is an example of what teachers call a 'What are you going to do about it letter?' in which all the onus for action is thrown on the school. This kind of matter is usually best dealt with by arranging a meeting where the problem can be fully discussed. It means that not too much is put on paper, and the matter can be sorted out. If the problem is taken over by a more senior member of staff, clarify what your role will be and make sure that you are kept informed of progress in case there are any ramifications which might involve you.

CASE STUDY 9.3. FOR ACTION

From your classroom window you see that Mr Page is waiting at the entrance for his daughter, Miranda. You know that Mr and Mrs Page have recently divorced and you are not sure what Mr Page's rights of access are. It is the second time this week that he has met her from school.

For action:

What is expected of you in this situation?
Is there a difference if Mr Page comes into your classroom and asks for Miranda?

Difficult Encounters

You will have some difficult encounters – all teachers do sooner or later. They can occur at a parents' meeting, at an interview in the school with parents or, most traumatically, when a parent erupts unexpectedly into school. Sometimes the kind of preparation described earlier in the chapter could have pre-empted the problem, but often the incident is sparked off by events you could not be expected to have anticipated.

If a parent wants to voice dissatisfaction, you will naturally be on the defensive. Some ploys you could use are:

- blame someone else, eg the child, inadequate resources, the governors, the government, etc.
- resort to technical language or jargon
- take a stance, eg teacher knows best.

Although such techniques as these may get the parents off your back for the time being, they are unlikely to work as long-term solutions, because they do not address the problem. Often the aggressive behaviour is the product of anxiety about their child or the home situation. Sometimes it is because some parents find it difficult to deal with schools and teachers. The best thing to do is to remain as calm as possible and try to find out what the main issue really is. If the outburst occurs at a parents' meeting, make it clear that this is not the place for a prolonged discussion and arrange a follow-up meeting which gives you time to prepare and to have someone experienced with you if necessary. S/he cannot simply interrupt a lesson and send a pupil for a member of the senior management team who could support you and find out what the problem is.

CASE STUDY 9.4. FOR ACTION

An unexpected visitor

The door opens and Mrs Jenks arrives in your classroom enraged. 'You've been picking on Freddy again,' she shouts. 'I won't have it!'

You are in the middle of a lesson with 9B, who are fascinated by this exciting development in a hitherto unexciting lesson.

For action:

How should you handle this sensitive situation?

The most difficult of all is probably the 'know it all'. Our advice here is don't try to be clever — it could rebound, and try not to get too irritated. If this kind of parent can't rile you, s/he is likely to move on to easier prey!

A difficult session with a parent can be upsetting and depressing. It is not unlike taking a difficult lesson. You will feel worse if you know that the incident could have been avoided, but it is important that, like a bad lesson, you keep its relative importance in proportion: don't get too upset and try to do better next time.

Always try to end a meeting with parents on a positive note, because this helps you build up the relationship with them. When the interview has gone as far as you feel you can get in that session, take the initiative in bringing it to an end. A good way of doing this is to sum up where you have reached, restate what each of you is going to do before the next meeting, and say clearly what you are hoping to achieve for the child. Establish what the timespan is so that you can avoid receiving the kind of letter, like letter 3, which accuses you of having done nothing since the meeting. Make a note afterwards of anything which requires follow up. Formally end the meeting by shaking hands with the parents and, if it seems appropriate, escort them to the door/entrance. In any follow-up communication, report progress and make a point of commenting favourably on any improvement.

How do you Contact a Parent?

CASE STUDY 9.5. FOR ACTION

Bobby never does his homework and generally seems to have his mind anywhere except on your lesson. You feel that a word with his parents could be useful, and you would like to clarify how many of Bobby's excuses are genuine and if problems outside school are affecting his concentration.

For action:

What is the procedure if, like Bobby's teacher, you want to contact a parent?

There are probably different answers to the question depending upon whether you work mainly in a primary or a secondary school. In a primary school you are usually a class teacher and much more likely to have regular contacts with parents, for example when they come to collect their child at the end of the day, and it can be possible to have an informal chat to a parent without having to write or telephone to make a special appointment. This kind of contact is rarely possible in a secondary school.

In a secondary school, it is most unlikely that you will make your own arrangements to see a set of parents and probably it would be unwise to do so. In case study 9.5 it was not clear whether Bobby's concentration was worse in your lesson than in other teachers', so the first step is always to see whether you are the only teacher experiencing this particular problem, and then to refer the matter to the year head or the form tutor, as appropriate. If it is then felt that a discussion with the parents is a good idea, the year head will make arrangements so, as a matter of principle, do not write to or phone parents on your own initiative or without consulting anyone. If you have agreed at the parents' meeting to report back to a set of parents about whether there has been any improvement, always inform the year head of arrangements of this sort. It would also be a sensible move to show the year head your draft letter before you send the progress report home.

Similarly, it is unlikely that you will be personally responsible for contacting EWOs or other agencies of this kind who work with pupils experiencing problems. If you think a pupil needs such help, consult those with pastoral responsibility for the pupil.

Parents as Helpers

Particularly in primary schools, parents are often invited into the classroom to work alongside children and teachers. At first you may be rather apprehensive or nervous about having parents in the room, especially if their children are members of the class, but they should not constitute a threat and you will quickly get used to their presence. A second pair of hands can be invaluable in a busy classroom, so do not spurn an offer of help from a parent. However, you need to make it work for you, and following the guidelines below could help you make effective use of parents who are willing to give up their time to assist you:

- find out what the school practice is in using parents as helpers and if necessary explain the rules to the parent
- ask colleagues how they organize parents in their classrooms
- ask your parent helpers what sort of tasks they enjoy and what their interests are
- make sure that you are prepared for the parents coming in and have organized a programme for them, eg attached them to specific pupils with clear tasks to carry out
- make them welcome when they arrive — remember that they are unpaid volunteers
- a briefing sheet might be helpful for the parents, especially in the first few lessons
- talk through with the parent/s what your learning objectives are, so that s/he understands what is happening in the lesson and make it clear where s/he fits into the scheme of things
- while you are addressing the whole class, the parent could be doing a job for you, eg setting out the equipment for the next stage in the lesson
- at the end of the session, take the time to have a few words with the parent, so that s/he doesn't feel like an intruder, and always remember to say thank you for their help!

CHAPTER 10

Keeping Sane

Stress

CASE STUDY 10.1. FOR ACTION

Yvonne Perkins, the deputy head in charge of the daily running of the school, looked at the absence sheet for the day and sighed. Laura Beckett was away again. Yvonne checked over the staff absence records for the past term. Yes, a pattern of absence was beginning to emerge. 'Either Laura was particularly prone to a gastric flu virus,' she thought, 'or we have a problem on our hands. I'd better have a word with her HOD, maybe he knows something that I don't'.

Laura was a modern languages teacher, and Mrs Perkins asked Roger Russell, the head of faculty, to come and see her. 'I'm a bit worried about Laura,' she said. 'The first year is always hard for an NQT, but she is looking extremely tired and strained. She looks very thin and I think she's losing weight, and I've noticed that Laura never seems to join the other members of the department when they sit and chat during the lunch hour, but just works by herself in the staff workbays. Now she is beginning to be away rather frequently. I've counted up the absences and I don't like what they suggest. Do you know if anything is wrong?'

Roger, who clearly thought that Mrs Perkins was fussing unduly, said that he hadn't noticed anything amiss with Laura. His own feeling was that she had a tendency to mistake mole hills for mountains and a difficulty with deadlines. Recently he hadn't found her very cooperative. 'I've given up my time to work with her and offered her a lot of advice, but she doesn't seem willing to take it. I really don't think she can see the wood for its trees,' he said, but he offered to 'have a word' with Laura. After a slight hesitation, Yvonne Perkins agreed. In theory this procedure was less threatening for

Laura than if Yvonne intervened personally, but Yvonne was all too aware that Roger was not the soul of tact and she was rather dubious about the outcome of his having a word with Laura. However, it was his job and she felt that he should carry it out.

An extremely public row followed, because Roger's well-meant, but insensitive, inquiry provoked Laura into flaring up at him and she ran out of the staffroom in floods of tears. Someone fetched Mrs Perkins, who found Laura sobbing in the staff cloakroom. She removed the NQT to the privacy of the deputy head's office, where she administered coffee and tissues and tried to find out what it was all about, because clearly something was badly wrong.

'Please don't think that I am just skiving off work, I'm not, really,' said Laura, tearfully. 'I just keep getting the same virus back over and over again. I don't seem to be able to shake it off.' The deputy sent Laura to see her doctor, who examined her and said that her run down and depressed condition was stress-related, and seemed to be arising from her concerns about work. 'Get the job sorted out and you will be fine,' he said.

'So what do I do now?', Laura asked Mrs Perkins. 'Being ill is affecting how I work, but I won't get better until I feel that I am on top of the job. If I'm ill all the time, I'll never be an effective teacher. It seems hopelessly circular to me.'

For action/discussion:

What are the main issues involved in this case study?
What advice would you give Laura and for what reasons?
How should this problem be resolved?

This case study highlights NQT stress. In recent years there has been recognition that teachers all too frequently suffer from stress. This condition has been defined as 'A response of negative effect (such as anger or depression) by the teacher resulting from aspects of the teachers' job ...' (Kyriacou and Sutcliffe, 1978). It is the body's reaction to a difficult or threatening situation and is usually associated with fear, anxiety, frustration, tension or conflict. How far an individual can cope with the ever expanding, constantly changing and highly challenging demands of teaching as a career will obviously vary, but research (for example, Coates and Thoreson, 1976) indicates that new entrants to the profession tend to show high levels of stress because they have not yet developed coping skills.

In the case study above, Laura is showing some of the classic symptoms of stress which will have an adverse effect upon her performance as a teacher:

- always tired and looking it – fatigue/exhaustion
- tense and strained
- weight loss – a result of poor appetite or not sleeping
- poor personal organization – eg difficulty with deadlines
- uncommunicative – drops out of social life of staffroom
- loss of detachment – can't see the wood for the trees
- irritable/unable to avoid confrontations – row with Roger
- unwillingness to listen, lack of cooperation/job avoidance
- illness – debilitating virus and the same condition recurs
- absence from work.

What kind of situation is likely to cause an NQT to become so stressed, and why are NQTs at such a high risk of stress?

The main causes of teacher stress are illustrated in Figure 10.1. As an NQT you are particularly at risk because many of the possible causes are likely to occur together when you take up a new post. Starting out in teaching is stressful because you have to adapt to a totally new situation. Most people find it difficult to cope with change and in a new post you will have developed fewer coping strategies than later on in your career.

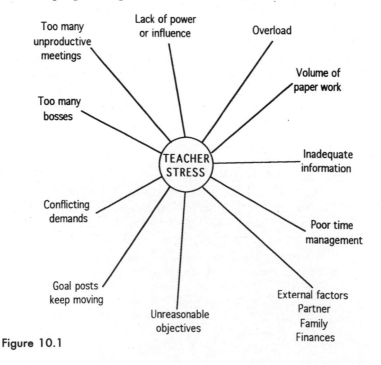

Figure 10.1

Causes of NQT Stress

Pressure/volume of work
As a new teacher you will have to prepare new courses for all the groups that you will have to teach and this involves a great deal of work. An NQT may be able to draw on lessons prepared for teaching practice, but the organization of groups, materials needed and the departmental approach may be quite different from those used in your teaching practice schools. As a result preparation can be very time-consuming in the first year of teaching.

Too many bosses
Teachers often work in more than one department, eg RS and English. Both departments will make demands of you and expect you to undertake tasks for them. There may also be a faculty head. On top of this, there will be a pastoral manager/year head with his/her own agenda to satisfy. You may have to fit into several teams and work to more than one line manager and to satisfy multiple, and sometimes conflicting, expectations. Too many bosses can put an NQT under pressure because s/he is likely to be anxious to fulfil all these expectations.

Relationship problems
In a new teaching post there are a lot of relationships to form. You have to fit in with your colleagues and also form relationships with the pupils. This is quite stressful in itself and all kinds of teaching problems and tensions can emerge which could also contribute to stress.

Lack of confidence
Anxiety lest you get things wrong, combined with over-estimating the importance of an individual unsuccessful lesson can cause loss of confidence and low self-esteem. Lack of success, apparent or real, can be a major cause of stress and lead to deteriorating relationships with students and performance in the classroom.

Unrealistic objectives
With so much preparation to carry out, so many bosses and a strong desire to prove yourself a good member of staff, it is all too easy to take on too much work or to set unrealistic objectives. Failing to meet the objectives can be a depressing experience.

Difficulties with line management

Meeting deadlines which affect other people, eg getting your reports completed on time or coping with pressure points of the school year, when all the major and time-consuming activities seem to come about in the same week, can put you under a lot of pressure. The number of meetings you have to attend can also erode the time you have available to do other work.

Lack of power

As an NQT you are back at the bottom of the heap – lowest in the pecking order of authority; most likely to have your authority questioned by pupils; and with variable ability, depending how democratic your school or department is, to influence any decisions made. This can be extremely frustrating.

Lack of information

Difficulty in getting hold of important information which enables you to do the job well is a common problem in teaching. As a new teacher, you may find difficulty in getting access to information and even in working out what you need to know. There can also be problems in determining the implications of what you have been told. You may find similar problems with access to resources or equipment. This can be both frustrating and time-consuming and could affect your performance.

External factors

Teaching does not happen in a vacuum. All kinds of external problems could contribute to stress and frequently do. Problems at home – your car won't work, you are having problems with your accommodation, your partner is unsympathetic to the amount of time you have to spend on preparation, your partner loses his/her job, your parents are sick – all affect how much time you can give to the job and how well you are likely to cope with its demands and pressures. If you are stressed at home, you are unlikely to regard a problem at school as a challenge or react to it positively.

CASE STUDY 10.2. FOR REFLECTION

We return to the case of Laura, the NQT whose symptoms were described in case study 10.1. When the deputy head probed into the situation, a saga of pressure of work, anxiety for her classes to do well, insecurity in the classroom, difficulties in meeting school deadlines, school functions eroding her free time and problems with her landlady, rapidly emerged.

She had lost her appetite altogether, wasn't sleeping well and now kept getting gastric flu. Roger's intervention was simply the last straw: 'He says he wants to help me, but really it's just an excuse to tell me what a good teacher he is, and that I've done it all wrong, yet again,' she said. Clearly the relationship with Roger, her HOD, left much to be desired and there was tension between them. He claimed that he is giving her advice, but that she is not willing to listen; she found the sessions with him very discouraging. These unsuccessful sessions obviously ate into her free time when she was already working through her lunch hour, losing out on social contacts and returning to the classroom in the afternoon unrefreshed. All this would affect how lively and interesting a teacher she is, and how fast or well she can react to problems when they occur.

For Laura, her first six months teaching had meant a lot of hard work with no certainty that she was succeeding or that she would ever get on top of things. It was no wonder she was depressed. For Laura, anxiety, fatigue and lack of encouragement from her HOD have brought about depression, illness and the feeling that there was no light at the end of the tunnel.

For reflection:

What strategies can an NQT adopt in order to avoid stress or to deal with it when it occurs? (Some strategies are shown in Figure 10.2.)

Strategies for Dealing with Stress

Using the Problem-solving Approach

One approach could be to apply a problem-solving model and work through the stages. The one used here is based on the Rank Xerox model and can be applied to any difficult problem or situation. It is useful because it helps you to stand back from whatever difficult situation you are in and take a more detached approach.

1. Recognize and Assess the Problem

This involves taking a close look at what the problem is about, analysing it, working out what the main issues are and breaking it

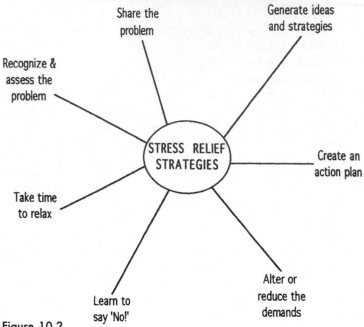

Figure 10.2

down into its component parts. Problems often become more manageable when they are tackled in clearly defined stages, so don't be tempted to skip the analysis stage and jump straight to the solutions. Defining the problem helps you to suggest possible avenues for action. Analyse whether your problem is mainly personal, departmental or institutional. Is it about time, relationships, resources or what? Think about who else is involved and consider the viewpoints of the different people concerned. Analysing the problem usually helps to put it into perspective.

2. Share the Problem

It is important to remember that you are not on your own. In Chapter 2 we described the mentoring system. If this works as it should, it will provide you with someone more experienced than you with whom you can discuss your problems and who will be more objective about things than you. Using your mentor effectively is an obvious way to relieve the pressure on you. What happens, however, if your school doesn't operate a mentor system, or if, like Laura, your relationship with your line manager is not going well? Although it might feel a bit like telling tales, it is important not to keep a problem to yourself, as it is more likely to increase rather than diminish. The member of the senior management team with responsibility for staff matters/staff development is the person to consult. He or she will either deal with it, or suggest someone suitable. A mentor or a critical friend can help you work your way through the problem and support you in dealing with it.

3. Generate Ideas/Suggest Strategies

Once you are clear what the issues are, the next step is to generate ideas to help you solve the problem. Having a critical friend to work with you at this stage may help you get started and assess the viability of the solutions. There is no blueprint for what will work. You have to start from the situation that you face, work out what the possibilities are and think about who can help you. Breaking the problem up into its component parts means that you can tackle the parts separately if necessary.

Sometimes you have to start by nibbling around the edges of the problem and leaving the more difficult or complex parts until you have built up your confidence through success, and you may have to be pragmatic and simply deal with what you can do now. At other times there is no alternative but to tackle the central issue before you can deal with the side-shows. You may find that you need to think in terms of short-term expedients and longer-term objectives.

4. Create an Action Plan

This is important as it gives you a formula to work to with your objectives or targets clearly set out for you. However, don't adhere to it so rigidly that it creates a new set of problems. It is a very good morale booster to be able to notch up success in achieving targets. This means that you have to make sure that your targets are realistic and achievable.

5. Alter or Reduce the Demands

Time pressures, overload and ever-increasing demands are a major cause of teacher stress. New teachers are no exception: for you, the preparation and marking can become synonymous with overload. You may need to think about what is a realistic amount to do in the time available rather than attempting, for example, to mark every piece of pupil work with the same degree of thoroughness. This may mean that you should review how efficiently you manage your time. Do you get straight to work or does it take you a while to get started? How much time do you waste this way? What proportion of your time is spent on each type of activity?

Monitoring how you spend your time over a week can help you think about ways of saving time. This technique involves keeping a diary, and it is important to be honest about what you do. Allied to this is the point made above about breaking tasks down into 'bite-sized chunks', achievable units, rather than setting yourself targets which don't relate to the time available or your degree of expertise.

6. Learn to Say No

It is always difficult to say no. In your first year or so of teaching, you don't want to create the impression that you are rude, uncooperative, or work-shy, but saying no occasionally is an important factor in avoiding stress. What matters here is when and to what you should say no. For example, don't agree to take on other major activities at times when you know that you will be pressurized, by examination marking or by reports and the like.

7. Learn to Turn Off – Take Time to Relax

There are techniques which can help you if you are experiencing stress. All work and no play is a recipe for stress and to deal with it people often resort to alcohol, cigarettes and sleeping pills. These palliatives are very short-term solutions and bring their own attendant problems. A healthy diet and regular meals are much more productive. Don't cut one meal and then overeat later, don't rely on coffee to keep the adrenalin running and, if possible, do relax for a short time before a meal.

It is very important to leave aside some time in the week or weekend for relaxation, as this helps you escape from the pressures of the job. You may find that a different challenge helps you to cope with work. Although competitive sports can bring their own pressures, regular exercise will release pent-up energy and improve the efficiency of the body. Swimming or jogging, approached with moderation, can be therapeutic. You need to let go both mentally and physically. Yoga and relaxation exercises can help, but a relaxing or creative hobby can do as much good in helping you keep things in perspective. So when you think that pressure of work means you haven't time for any of these things, remember that taking a reasonable amount of time off will help you keep things in proportion and will actually make you a better and more effective teacher.

CASE STUDY 10.3. FOR REFLECTION

How could the strategies described above help Laura, the NQT described earlier in this chapter?

Sharing the Problem

In this case, although Laura's relationship with her HOD was not good and she does not seem to have had a mentor, she did have access to help and advice, as Yvonne Perkins, the deputy head, had already begun to assume a support role. Yvonne had noticed the symptoms of distress and had begun to probe into the causes of Laura's depressed state. She would need to continue to support Laura and to use her counselling skills to help Laura to talk through the problem. Airing the problem is often the first step towards relieving stress.

Using the Problem-solving Model

Talking it through helped to clarify the problem. It was a mark of the progress they had made that Laura identified her own anxiety to succeed as the central issue. It had spurred her on to work long hours; it had led to a policy of perfectionism in preparation and marking; it had caused her to set the pupils the maximum number of homework assignments; it had made her pressurize the pupils; it had affected the type of activity she had undertaken with classes; it had made it difficult for her to relax; it had meant that she didn't participate in staffroom gossip and activities; it had affected her appetite and she had skipped meals; and it was keeping her awake at night.

Her relationship problem with Roger, her HOD, seemed to have resulted partially from the central issue of her anxiety about her performance. Roger had a reputation as a good teacher and she knew that she was not in his league, and might never be. His confidence affected hers adversely. She lacked the confidence to try to do things his way, and as he seemed to give her no credit for her hard work and effort, she began to be increasingly discouraged by the sessions with him and to dread them. Roger's reputation as a classroom teacher was not matched by any great skill as a manager of staff, but he noticed Laura's lack of enthusiasm and came to view her attitude as negative; thus relations between them had progressively deteriorated.

Generating Ideas

It was important to show Laura that her problems were not insurmountable and that support was available, so Mrs Perkins helped her identify some areas in which she could help herself or be helped:

- Replace the sessions with Roger by a more sympathetic mentor. Laura clearly needed support, but her mentor needed to be someone with whom she could relate and talk freely, and who would provide her with the encouragement she badly needed. What she needed was a critical friend.
- Cut down the workload. Over-anxiety had made Laura try to do too much. She had to review her workload and decide what her priorities were and plan out her week.
- Be sensible about health and meals. Mrs Perkins insisted initially on two main rules to help Laura back to health. She was not to cut out meals – some lunch and a short break in the lunch hour was to be compulsory and Yvonne would monitor this through to the end of term. She was not to work for at least the last 40 minutes before she went to bed each night, so that worries about school were not at the forefront of her mind when she tried to sleep. Mrs Perkins also suggested that next term Laura joined the staff keep-fit group.

Result

Mrs Perkins suggested to Roger, as tactfully as she could, that it would be better if his second in department, Frances, dealt with Laura and became her mentor. She briefed Frances very thoroughly about what was needed and the mentor encouraged Laura and helped her review how she approached her teaching. Things did not change overnight, but Laura's depression began to lift.

She took the advice about marking and time management, and spent time with Frances addressing this problem. Deadlines remained difficult, but became less of an nightmare.

Under Mrs Perkins' strict supervision, Laura regained a little weight and more resilience, and gradually began to develop more resistance to gastric flu. Her attendance steadily improved.

Mrs Perkins sent Roger on a management course to develop his interpersonal skills. She is dubious about its success.

CASE STUDY 10.4. FOR ACTION

There are so many pressures. I didn't realize that the job would be like this. It's a small department, so I have a lot of classes. There are so many names to learn and books to mark. Follow up is very difficult. RS is not a status subject and for most of the children it's not a priority, so I have to work really hard at making it attractive and this takes an enormous amount of time and effort. Almost every evening seemed to be spent on marking or preparation and tiredness has become an ongoing condition which depresses me a lot.

I found the A Level preparation particularly demanding and, after a while, I began to feel that the sixth formers were watching me to see how I coped with the difficult questions. They challenged me persistently and I suspected that it was becoming a game for them, to see what I said and if I got the answer right.

The effort that I had to put into A Level preparation affected how much time I could spend on creating the kind of Year 8 or 9 lesson which would motivate our lively and demanding pupils. They have become very difficult to control, and I have come to dread the weekly lessons with some Year 9 groups.

Worst of all, I have to contribute to the whole-school assembly programme, and I really hate this. It can take a whole evening to prepare an assembly, and, as exhaustion set in, I began to develop a real phobia about the moment I would have to walk down the centre aisle and onto the platform. I knew the children would fidget or cough in the way that they don't do for the head or deputy, and I have nightmares about the day when they will really misbehave, as I don't know what I shall do or how my colleagues will react. (Gavin, NQT.)

For action/discussion:

What are the issues involved in this case study?
What advice would you give Gavin a) in the short term, and b) in the
long term and on what grounds?
How can the school support Gavin?

CHAPTER 1

What Makes a Good Teacher?

> The essence of being an effective teacher lies in knowing what to do to foster pupils' learning and being able to bring it about. (Kryriacou, 1991.)

Every teacher wants to be effective — a successful practitioner — but what is effective teaching and how do you recognize it? We can all point to at least one colleague who is an effective teacher, and to another who is not, yet when it comes to pinning down precisely what this means, we find it very difficult, particularly since sometimes the concept is confused with the individual. Effective teaching is an extensively used, high profile and loaded concept, but one with few clear definitions. This is not because academics and practising teachers have not given thought to this issue, but rather because there are no easy answers to the question and no obvious blueprint for success. So how do you know:

- What is effective teaching?
- Whether you are being effective?
- How effective you are being?
- Where you stand in relation to colleagues?
- How to become more effective?

The Profile of an Effective Teacher

In the period since the 1960s studies have been carried out in both America and Britain which have tried to clarify what it means to be an effective teacher, but on the whole these have tended to muddy rather than clear the waters. For example, Brameld (1965) states that to be effective, a teacher should be, 'Creative, audacious, convergent, committed, confronting, involved and controlling'. Most NQTs would find that advice extremely difficult to follow.

Because of the problem of defining effective teaching, the surveys undertaken in the 1980s have largely concentrated on identifying what constitutes teaching skills. Noticeable is the Teacher Education Project led by Professor Ted Wragg, which attempted to analyse particular skills in relation to broad areas of activity, ie class management, mixed ability teaching, questioning and explaining. This project roughly defined teaching skills as, 'repeatable strategies that teachers used which facilitated pupils' learning'.

Kyriacou's work, mentioned at the beginning of this chapter, takes this kind of approach to its logical conclusion. In his very useful book, *Essential Teaching Skills* (1991), he analyses the features of successful teaching and identifies seven essential skills:

■ Planning and preparation
The skills involved in selecting the educational aims and learning outcomes intended for a lesson, and how to achieve these.

■ Lesson presentation
The skills involved in successfully engaging pupils in the learning experience, particularly in relation to the quality of instruction.

■ Lesson management
The skills involved in managing and organizing the learning activities taking place during the lesson to maintain the pupils' attention, interest and involvement.

■ Classroom climate
The skills involved in establishing and maintaining positive attitudes and motivation by pupils towards the lesson.

■ Discipline
The skills involved in maintaining good order and dealing with pupil misbehaviour when it occurs.

■ Assessing pupil progress
The skills involved in assessing pupil progress, covering both formative (ie, intended to aid pupils' future development) and summative (ie, providing a record of attainment) purposes of assessment.

■ Reflection and evaluation

The skills involved in evaluating one's own current practice in order to improve future practice.

If you master these skills you are likely to become an effective teacher, but with the emphasis that is currently being put on 'quality of teaching' in all recent legislation and DfE pronouncements, it seems necessary to probe further. The OFSTED guidance given in *Framework for Inspection* (1991) provides a clear clue for current thinking. For example, '6.1 Quality of Teaching' spells out what is acceptable and what OFSTED regards as unsatisfactory. First it deals with good teaching:

> WHERE TEACHING IS GOOD pupils acquire knowledge, skills and understanding progressively and at a good pace. The lessons have clear aims and purposes. They cater appropriately for the learning of pupils of differing abilities and interests and ensure the full participation of all. The teaching methods suit the topic or subject as well as the pupils; the conduct of the lesson signals high expectations of all pupils and sets high but attainable challenges. There is regular feedback which helps pupils make progress, both through thoughtful marking and discussion of work with pupils. Relationships are positive and promote pupils' motivation. National Curriculum Attainment Targets and programmes of study are fully taken into account. Where appropriate, homework which extends or complements the work done in lessons is set regularly.

Then it describes unsatisfactory teaching:

> TEACHING IS UNSATISFACTORY where pupils fail to achieve standards commensurate with their potential. The teaching is ill-prepared or unclear. Pupils are unable to see the point of what they are being asked to do. They are not appropriately challenged, nor are they helped to form a useful assessment of their level of attainment and of what needs to be improved. Specific learning needs of individuals in the class are not recognised sufficiently. Relationships are insecure and inhibit learning.

What it seems to come down to is that you have to ask yourself, 'What are the things that I have to get right in order to be a good teacher?' Analysis of the OFSTED guidance and reflection on what constitutes good practice suggest that there are about a dozen essential features of good quality teaching. It is perhaps easier to express these ideas as a diagram than to try to list them; and this we have done in Figure 11.1.

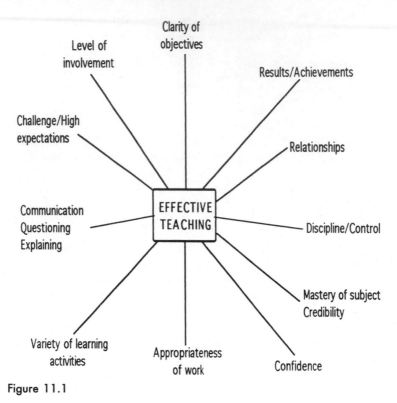

Figure 11.1

Evaluating Your Work

Evaluation is a form of critical thinking about one's performance on the job. Once you have started teaching you will very soon find that teachers spend a lot of time reflecting on their practice and trying to improve. Most of this evaluation is extremely informal; for example, at the end of a lesson most teachers say to themselves, 'That went well' or, 'That went badly'. This is a simple form of self-evaluation about how you have performed and is almost a daily process in schools. Similarly departments regularly discuss how a particular activity has worked with different sets – again this is a very simple form of evaluation, but both these examples could serve as the first step in a more stringent process.

Often reflection upon one's performance in the classroom is sparked off by the need to react to a specific problem that has arisen or by your participation in a new initiative where regular monitoring is an essential part of the project. Mentoring student teachers or NQTs frequently acts as a catalyst for reflection and evaluation of personal practice and for this reason some schools encourage as many staff as possible to gain experience of mentoring. The most formal evaluation takes place as part of your appraisal process or as an action research project with specific focuses and clearly defined objectives and targets.

If you want to evaluate how well you are doing, how should you set about it? The evaluation process should include:

- selecting the focus
- collecting the evidence
- analysing the data
- discussing the issues with your mentor or a colleague
- suggesting strategies
- formulating targets for the future
- devising strategies for achieving the targets.

Selecting the Focus

There is no need to evaluate everything you do. You will want to select a particular aspect of your teaching as a focus for evaluation. What you choose usually arises out of a perceived need or particular problem that you are experiencing. When choosing a focus, make it specific and not too general; clarify your objectives and make sure that they are achievable.

Collecting the Evidence

There are a number of methods of collecting data. You can employ them either separately or together.

Observation – this is the main means of judging how a teacher teaches. Appraisal now demands a minimum of an hour's observation in two separate sessions. Lesson observation is most effective where a particular feature, such as questioning/handling of group work is targeted, as it is difficult for the observer to watch and assess everything in a lesson.

Documents – eg, lesson plans/marking schemes. These indicate the intentions/objectives you set yourself and the appraiser can test these against what actually happens in a lesson and make a judgement about how far the objectives have been communicated, understood and achieved. You can also use this method to assess how thoroughly a lesson was planned and where and how well it fits into a sequence.

Written work from a sample of pupils – this can show how far the tasks are appropriate and the way in which the pupils have responded to them. Sampling written work will also indicate how consistently the work is marked and what proportion is done as homework.

Talking to pupils – this is a very useful activity as it will indicate how the pupils have perceived the session and provide evidence about their level of involvement/attitude which may not have emerged in the lesson. Talking to pupils will also provide evidence about how they think they are progressing. Some subjects build into their syllabus regular feedback sessions with groups of pupils, for instance at the end of a topic. This is good practice because it makes it a normal feature rather than an unusual event, which could affect the quality of the pupils' contributions.

Discussions with the teacher – this is a valuable method of establishing the teacher's intentions and how s/he perceived the lesson. It is also a helpful means of putting the lesson in context.

Recording – either through diary entries made by the teacher and pupils immediately after the lesson, or by videoing a lesson or part of a lesson. Keeping a diary is a useful way of helping you clarify issues and concerns. Videoing your lesson allows you to see yourself teach.

Observation is clearly central to evaluating teaching, but the other methods supplement and enhance what can be learnt.

Analysing the Data

You will have acquired a lot of data; now you have to analyse and interpret them. This entails examining the data to see whether:

- a pattern emerges
- your perception of how you teach matches that of the observer of the pupils
- the data confirm your expectations
- there are any major surprises.

Discussing the Issues with your Mentor or a Colleague

In a number of chapters in this book (for example, Chapters 2 and 10) we have recommended that you do not try to work things out entirely alone and that a support structure should exist to help you. Once you have completed the data collection, the next step is to discuss the issues which arise from the data collection through with your mentor or HOD, evaluate what you have achieved and work on formulating the targets together.

Suggesting Strategies and Formulating Targets for the Future

Your reflection on your practice should be formative rather than summative and should not end with summarizing what was good and what was weak in the aspect of teaching examined in the evaluation. Rather, it should lead onto the devising strategies for improving your practice in the future. Evaluation is about 'Where am I now?', but you need to work out how you can do the job better. A brainstorming session where you raise ideas and assess their merits is usually the best way to approach what you should do next; the mentoring system lends itself to enabling this, because a good mentor will help you formulate your targets.

Improving Your Teaching

On the whole it is not true that good teachers are born and not made. Some teachers are naturally better than others, but most can improve their practice with determination and application. Effective methods can be learnt. Reflective practice means that you are constantly thinking about and evaluating your teaching. The ideas that follow depend upon this approach.

- Build evaluation into your teaching cycle and act upon it.
- Share experience through discussions with colleagues.
- Observe an experienced colleague teaching something you find difficult and then analyse the techniques used.
- Take advantage of coaching by your mentor or HOD.
- Take on board the training targeted to specific needs, eg teaching Shakespeare or strategies for group work via courses or department-based Inset.
- Use case studies as the basis for analysis of issues and discussion of strategies.

A simple but effective idea is to continue to use the kind of lesson debriefing sheet you may have used at college. Use it occasionally to assess your own practice and set yourself targets for the next time you teach that lesson or series of lessons.

CASE STUDY 11.1. FOR DISCUSSION/REFLECTION

Pupil feedback

Feedback from pupils, whether in the form of written questionnaires, commentaries or discussion with individuals or groups, can be very useful. However, some teachers feel threatened by it, because they fear it is like taking the stopper out of a bottle which will unleash a plethora of pupil complaint, or they fear that they will not be able to adapt the lesson in the way the pupils suggest.

If the feedback is wholly critical, then there is all the more need to review the activity. If you can't do what the pupils suggest, you will obviously have to explain why not and the reasons for your chosen approach.

Another fear is that pupil feedback is of limited value because many will write or say what they think you want to hear. Of course there will always be a few pupils of this type, but if you use this approach regularly, the pupils will get used to it; if it is used as one of a number of methods of collecting evidence, it will be clear where it fits in the scheme of things.

Sometimes the feedback is so positive that it will give you a real boost. The example in Figure 11.2 is of this type. Most of the case studies used in this book have been examples of things going wrong, so that you could analyse the issues involved and work out how to rectify the situation, but it is also important to taste the good things of teaching and getting through to an individual or group of pupils can be very good indeed. It can be difficult to analyse good practice because the strands are crafted together so that it is difficult to disentangle them.

Here the group have been asked for their reactions to a simulation exercise undertaken in the previous lesson. All the responses were very positive and the example given here has been chosen because this pupil has responded to the activity with such enthusiasm that s/he cannot think of any reason why simulations could fail to enthuse a class. What more could any teacher want!

Human emotions are often a key factor in what has created the History we study today. To understand History you need to understand the situation faced by people of the time. Trying to avoid or create a situation or system often helps to understand the actions of the characters you are portraying in a role-play.

Role-play simulations take you mentally out of the classroom into another era, they are excitingly interactive with other students, compared to the drudgery of a book and pen. Simulations are immensely enjoyable especially if you like acting and drama, even if you lack confidence, the role-plays are amusing and helpful.

A classroom of students can easily represent the most cataclysmic events. A simulation is a perfect way to remember facts for exams, the memory of a classmate's reaction to a situation is an easier image to remember than a paragraph of writing.

Simulations are exciting and bring History to life. They are anticipated enthusiastically by all students who hate the grey nothing that is sometimes text and notes. Role-plays often centre on the bleaker areas of History that the national curriculum has provided but the chance to talk, to act, to understand and have immense fun outweighs this.

My best memory of our work on post revolutionary Russia is when a friend and I sentenced the entire class of Kulaks, intellectuals and party members to death as part of Stalin's purges. It brought across to me especially how easy it was to hold someone's life in the balance, towards the end I even began to feel guilty. But this feeling did not last when our teacher ended the simulation by sending my fellow judge and me for execution.

For reflection/discussion:

Why has the pupil enjoyed this activity so much?
What does s/he see as the value of the activity?
What are the lessons of this case study for you as an NQT?

Bibliography

Barnes, D (1976) *From Communication to Curriculum*, Harmondsworth: Penguin.

Benton, P (1981) 'Writing how it is received', in *Communicating in the Classroom*, London: Hodder & Stoughton.

Brameld, T (1965) *Education as Power*, New York: Holt, Rinehart and Winston.

Brown, GA and Armstrong, S (1984) 'Explaining and explanations', in Wragg, E (ed.) *Classroom Teaching Skills*, Beckenham: Croom Helm.

Brown, GA and Edmondson, R (1984) 'Asking questions', in Wragg, E (ed.) *Classroom Teaching Skills*, Beckenham: Croom Helm.

Coates, TJ and Thoreson, CE (1976) 'Teacher anxiety – a review with recommendations', *Review of Educational Research*, Vol 46 (2).

Howe, D (1993) *Into the Classroom*, Tamworth: Bracken Press.

Kerry, T (1982) The DES Education Project Focus Series, Basingstoke: Macmillan. Includes such titles as:
Brown, G and Hatton, N, *Explanations and Explaining*
Kerry, T, *The New Teacher*
Kerry, T, *Effective Questioning*
Kerry, T and Sands, MK, *Handling Classroom Groups*
Wragg, E, *Classroom Management and Control*

Kounin, J (1970) *Discipline and Group Management in Classrooms*, New York: Holt, Rinehart and Winston.

Kyriacou, C (1991) *Essential Teaching Skills*, London: Simon and Shuster.

Kyriacou, C and Sutcliffe, J (1978) 'A model of teacher stress', *Education Studies*, vol 4, March.

Marland, M (1975) *The Craft of the Classroom*, Oxford: Heinemann.

Marlow, C (1994) *Beginning to Teach, Primary Teaching Explained*, London: David Fulton.

OFSTED (1991) *A Framework for Inspection*, London: HMSO.

Richardson, E (1973) *The Environment of Learning*, Oxford: Heinemann.

Rutter, M, Maughan, B, Mortimore, P and Ouston, J (1979) *Fifteen Thousand Hours*, Wells: Open Books.

Sutton, C (ed.) (1981) *Communicating in the Classroom*, London: Hodder & Stoughton.

Tanner, L (1978) *Classroom Discipline*, New York: Holt, Rinehart and Winston.

Trethowan, D (1985) *Teamwork in Schools*, Management in Schools Series, London: The Industrial Society.

Wheldall, K (1989) and Glynn, T *Effective Classroom Learning*, Oxford: Blackwell.

Wragg, E (1984) *Classroom Teaching Skills*, Beckenham: Croom Helm.

Index